Student Outcomes Assessment: What Institutions Stand to Gain

Diane F. Halpern, *Editor*
California State University, San Bernardino

NEW DIRECTIONS FOR HIGHER EDUCATION
MARTIN KRAMER, *Editor-in-Chief*
University of California, Berkeley

Number 59, Fall 1987

Paperback sourcebooks in
The Jossey-Bass Higher Education Series

Jossey-Bass Inc., Publishers
San Francisco • London

Diane F. Halpern (ed.).
Student Outcomes Assessment: What Institutions Stand to Gain.
New Directions for Higher Education, no. 59.
Volume XV, number 3.
San Francisco: Jossey-Bass, 1987.

New Directions for Higher Education
Martin Kramer, *Editor-in-Chief*

New Directions for Higher Education is published quarterly
by Jossey-Bass Inc., Publishers (publication number USPS
990-880). *New Directions* is numbered sequentially—please
order extra copies by sequential number. The volume and issue
numbers above are included for the convenience of libraries.
Second-class postage paid at San Francisco, California, and at
additional mailing offices. POSTMASTER: Send address changes to
Jossey-Bass Inc., Publishers, 433 California Street, San Francisco,
California 94104.

Editorial correspondence should be sent to the Editor-in-Chief,
Martin Kramer, 2807 Shasta Road, Berkeley, California 94708.

Library of Congress Catalog Card Number LC 85-644752

International Standard Serial Number ISSN 0271-0560

International Standard Book Number ISBN 1-55542-949-1

Cover art by WILLI BAUM

Manufactured in the United States of America

Ordering Information

The paperback sourcebooks listed below are published quarterly and can be ordered either by subscription or single copy.

Subscriptions cost $48.00 per year for institutions, agencies, and libraries. Individuals can subscribe at the special rate of $36.00 per year *if payment is by personal check*. (Note that the full rate of $48.00 applies if payment is by institutional check, even if the subscription is designated for an individual.) Standing orders are accepted.

Single copies are available at $11.95 when payment accompanies order. (California, New Jersey, New York, and Washington, D.C., residents please include appropriate sales tax.) For billed orders, cost per copy is $11.95 plus postage and handling.

Substantial discounts are offered to organizations and individuals wishing to purchase bulk quantities of Jossey-Bass sourcebooks. Please inquire.

Please note that these prices are for the academic year 1987–88 and are subject to change without notice. Also, some titles may be out of print and therefore not available for sale.

To ensure correct and prompt delivery, all orders must give either the *name of an individual* or an *official purchase order number*. Please submit your order as follows:

    Subscriptions: specify series and year subscription is to begin.
    Single Copies: specify sourcebook code (such as, HE1) and first two words of title.

Mail orders for United States and Possessions, Australia, New Zealand, Canada, Latin America, and Japan to:
    Jossey-Bass Inc., Publishers
    433 California Street
    San Francisco, California 94104

Mail orders for all other parts of the world to:
    Jossey-Bass Limited
    28 Banner Street
    London EC1Y 8QE

New Directions for Higher Education Series
Martin Kramer, *Editor-in-Chief*

HE1   *Facilitating Faculty Development*, Mervin Freedman
HE2   *Strategies for Budgeting*, George Kaludis
HE3   *Services for Students*, Joseph Katz

Contents

Editor's Notes

Interest in assessing student learning outcomes in higher education has burgeoned during the past five years. At last count, eleven state legislatures have mandated some sort of outcomes measures for every public postsecondary institution in those states, with countless private colleges and universities around the United States joining the outcomes assessment bandwagon. What are they all measuring, and how is the information being used? In an attempt to answer these and related questions, the Chancellor's Office of the California State University provided funding for a conference on student outcomes assessment, which was held at Kellogg West Conference Facilities in Pomona, California, October 15-17, 1986. Participants included faculty and administrators from each of the nineteen California State University campuses, legislative aides, the governor's education adviser, campus equity officers, and representatives from the California State Student Association, the University of California, California Community Colleges, the California Postsecondary Education Commission, as well as other interested individuals. This volume includes, in edited form, the proceedings of that conference.

The assessment of educational gains is a crucial issue in higher education throughout the United States. National interest in this topic is growing rapidly. The concept has been endorsed by the National Governors' Association, and several accrediting agencies have already begun to require some sort of outcomes measurement as part of the accrediting process. There is a clear need to understand the ramifications of outcomes assessment as an educational policy issue.

The chapters in this volume span a wide variety of issues and concerns about assessing student outcomes. In Part 1 and Chapter One, I begin with an overview of and introduction to the topics considered in this volume. Peter T. Ewell, in Chapter Two, shares a wealth of knowledge gleaned from his experience in virtually every type and size of postsecondary institution in the United States and Canada. In Chapter Three, William E. Vandament offers a perspective from a large state university system in which implementation of any systemwide program creates mammoth logistical problems. Lee Kerschner, in Chapter Four, discusses considerations in assessing student gains at all levels of higher education. Part 2 offers case studies from four diverse state institutions in Tennessee, Missouri, New Jersey, and Florida. The authors of these chapters have all been involved in planning and implementing the student outcomes assessment models used at their institutions. They tell us about their mistakes and their triumphs. In Part 3, Daniel P. Resnick and Marc Goulden

1

(Chapter Nine) review the history of assessment initiatives in the United States and Europe. Alexander W. Astin, in Chapter Ten, suggests ways of resolving the apparent conflict between state and institutional interests. The concluding chapter summarizes these topics and suggests guidelines and caveats for successful student outcomes assessment programs.

Diane F. Halpern
Editor

Diane F. Halpern is interim dean of undergraduate studies and professor of psychology at California State University, San Bernardino. She served as chair for the October 1986 conference entitled "Student Outcomes Assessment: A Tool for Improving Teaching and Learning," sponsored by the California State University.

Part 1.
The Case for Assessing
Student Outcomes
in Higher Education

State legislatures, taxpayers, students and their parents, accrediting agencies, national task forces, and private industry have all been pressuring postsecondary institutions to demonstrate that they are providing high-quality education. In response to mounting pressures for accountability and to genuine concern for educational excellence, the assessment of student outcomes has been growing in popularity. The purpose of student outcomes assessment is to provide an index of what and how much students are learning. Although assessment programs vary in their objectives and intended uses, most have focused on student gains in cognitive development, knowledge base, and such selected attitudes as esthetic appreciation and tolerance of differences.

The assessment of student outcomes is not new; most institutions have been engaging for some time in various forms of learner assessment and measures of institutional effectiveness, ranging from entry-level placement examinations to surveys of alumni and employers. What is new is that student outcomes assessment is now more coordinated and programmatic. Results are being used in strategic planning, to justify funding, to attract potential students, and to provide quality assurances to potential employers. The four chapters in Part 1 lay the basic foundation for understanding the contemporary issues in student outcomes assessment.

Is your university doing a good job of educating its students?
How do you know? Student outcomes assessment provides a
direct and valid way of answering these questions.

Student Outcomes Assessment: Introduction and Overview

Diane F. Halpern

Higher education has been the focus of considerable criticism in the last several years. Numerous national reports have questioned the *Integrity in the Curriculum,* have described us as *A Nation at Risk,* and have urged higher education *To Reclaim a Legacy.* These reports and others have decried the quality of undergraduate education. Private industry, prospective students and their families, faculty and administrators, the military, and state officials have joined the various task forces created to examine the status of higher education and have begun to demand evidence that the large and growing amount of public money being spent on higher education is producing educated adults.

In responding to our critics and to those clamoring for accountability, one problem we face is difficulty in defining quality. Usually we recognize superior universities by their research reputations and by the size and cost of their physical plants. By these criteria, only the large research institutions will be judged excellent, while small colleges and universities, especially those with major commitments to teaching undergraduates, are doomed to mediocre standing at best. Assessment of learning outcomes is one solution to this lopsided notion of educational quality. Instead of documenting excellence by variables unrelated to learning, like research reputation and size, or inferring quality by examining opinion

D. F. Halpern (ed.). *Student Outcomes Assessment: What Institutions Stand to Gain.*
New Directions for Higher Education, no. 59. San Francisco: Jossey-Bass, Fall 1987.

surveys, number of volumes in the library, and retention rates, we can assess educational quality more directly by examining what and how much students actually learn.

Definition of Terms

The many authors of the literature on student outcomes assessment rarely agree on the meanings of several key terms. Astin (Chapter Ten, this volume), for example, makes a distinction between value-added/talent development and outcomes measures. According to Astin, the terms *value-added* and *talent development* are often used synonymously to denote either the educational gains attributable to having spent time at a university or the amount and type of talent that an individual has developed as a result of university attendance. Thus, these are complementary terms that stress individual and group changes associated with university attendance. The term *learning outcomes measures* refers to measurement of how much an individual or a group of students may know upon completion of a degree program. Such measures are affected by how much students know when they enter an institution. Thus, the very brightest university freshmen are likely to be among the very brightest graduates, and the freshmen who are the most underprepared academically are likely to have the lowest class standings at graduation. The distinction made by Astin is a legitimate one, acknowledging that significant learning outcomes do not necessarily reflect the greatest educational gains, but it has not been adopted in the majority of the literature. For the purposes of this volume, the term *student outcomes assessment* will refer to the outcomes of higher education and can be used to reflect educational gains when appropriate comparisons are made between freshmen and seniors.

The Case for Assessing Outcomes

Using student outcomes assessment, institutions can refocus their priorities so that educational quality is based on what and how much students learn in school. Outcomes-focused attention allows institutions to determine the difference between where students are when they enter and where they are when they graduate. Net gains in knowledge and human understanding represent a better measure of a university's educational effectiveness than do more traditional measures, which rely on number of students served or amount of money spent.

An emphasis on student outcomes gives visible priority to undergraduate education. Outcomes assessment can be used as a diagnostic tool for counseling incoming students, so that they can be placed in appropriate classes and, if necessary, begin remedial work at the earliest possible time. Outcomes assessment can also serve as a stimulus for program change. It has been said that to change educational policies and programs is a lot like moving a graveyard: You don't get much internal support. The types of data examined in assessing student outcomes will enable institutions to assign priorities for improvement and to evaluate the impact of any changes made to achieve it. While outcomes assessment may not be able to save higher education from its critics, it is one way to respond to the growing demand for accountability from state legislatures, independent agencies, and taxpayers while also providing valuable feedback both to the student and to the university.

Models of Student Outcomes Assessment

Across North America, numerous postsecondary institutions and state legislatures have begun assessing student outcomes. The major difference from program to program is the intended primary use of the outcomes data. Although there are numerous subtle differences among the models, three major categories or typologies have emerged. In each model, data are used for a different purpose.

Program Improvement. Assessments of student outcomes are frequently used to provide information to individual students so that they can gauge their academic progress. When aggregated, the same information can be used to make programs (for example, academic major, general education, and certificate programs) more effective in meeting their goals and the overall mission of the institution. When colleges undertake outcomes assessment primarily for program improvement, procedures usually include diagnostic placement tests for incoming students and exit tests that allow students to measure the educational gains from their college years. Exit tests also provide normative information, so that graduates of a program can be compared to graduates from other, similar institutions.

A program-improvement emphasis requires active use by faculty and administrators of the information collected to effect change. There are a number of ancillary benefits to linking outcomes with curriculum improvement. Faculty are more supportive of change when they have participated in the assessment process and when the need for assessment is clearly documented. Improved programs not only produce better-educated students but also lead to greater student and faculty satisfaction and to improved retention rates. Apart from their educational benefits, high retention rates derived from improved programs are also cost-effective in maintaining enrollments. Thus, it may have indirect financial benefits as well.

Gatekeeping Functions. The purpose of assessment in "gateway" models is to ensure basic academic competencies in all graduates. In Florida's version (explained more completely in Chapter Eight), every sophomore in the state must pass a competency examination before advancing to junior status. The intent is laudable. There has been considerable concern that college graduates do not necessarily have basic skills and knowledge in writing and mathematics. This concern has led major employers, like IBM and the United States military, to begin remedial programs in these areas for the college graduates they employ. "Gateway" models are roughly analogous to industry's quality assurance models. The rationale in "gateway" models is that deficient students need to be screened before they begin upper-division coursework, in much the same way that deficient widgets are screened out of a production line.

Much of the criticism of outcomes assessment is directed at programs based on gatekeeping functions. One unintended negative consequence of Florida's model has been a devastating reduction in the number of Spanish-speaking students eligible to continue as college juniors. "Gateway" models pay the high price of abandoning the goals of educational equity, a price that some believe is too high for the benefit of reducing remediation at the upper-division level.

Budget Decisions and Accountability. The primary focus of an assessment program designed to assist in budget decisions and accountability is to determine whether taxpayers and parents are "getting their money's worth." Of course, there is no reason why information generated for these purposes cannot also be used for improving curricular offerings and student services. In Tennessee, for example, measures of improved student outcomes are used to help institutions qualify for incentive funding. As described in Chapter Five, individual campuses can receive up to 5 percent of additional funds (beyond what is generated by usual funding formulas) by demonstrating, among other things, academic achievement in general education and in majors.

Most outcomes assessment programs are undertaken for a variety of reasons. In fact, they may represent blends of these three typologies. The purposes and mechanics of assessing student outcomes are described in the following chapters, which include multiple models, as well as suggestions and caveats for successful programs.

Diane F. Halpern is interim dean of undergraduate studies and professor of psychology at California State University, San Bernardino. She served as chair for the October 1986 conference entitled "Student Outcomes Assessment: A Tool for Improving Teaching and Learning," sponsored by the California State University.

Determining an appropriate assessment approach is an art that depends on clear knowledge of what is intended, solid research about available instruments and about the experiences of other institutions, and an accurate diagnosis of the local organizational and political climate.

Establishing a Campus-Based Assessment Program

Peter T. Ewell

If this volume is viewed as a curriculum on the emerging topic of student outcomes assessment, this chapter is intended as its general education component. As such, its ends are by definition ambitious, and its contents are bound to be unsatisfying. The chapters that follow will illustrate, in a far more effective fashion than I can, the many conceptual and practical dilemmas involved in establishing a workable institutional approach to assessment. My hope here is to provide a coherent framework for comparing and evaluating these varied approaches.

In beginning this task, it is no longer necessary for me to justify a place for assessment on the agenda of issues facing higher education. Recent events have provided ample evidence of its power to provoke public discussion, and identifiable institutional assessment programs are no longer novel. A major hallmark of assessment efforts continues to be their diversity. Institutional approaches range from those that emphasize periodic assessment of student goal attainment and job placement to those centered on cognitive gains achieved by students in different curricula to those that seek to change the structure of teaching and learning in individual classrooms. Indeed, the definition of *assessment* continues to vary according to who uses the term for what purpose and in what political context.

D. F. Halpern (ed.). *Student Outcomes Assessment: What Institutions Stand to Gain.*
New Directions for Higher Education, no. 59. San Francisco: Jossey-Bass, Fall 1987.

This situation creates a challenge for an institution embarking on assessment. The present chapter is one attempt to sort through that challenge by identifying the relevant institution-specific choices that need to be addressed. Two key concepts will run throughout this discussion. The first is the notion of choice itself. No assessment approach can successfully investigate all possible outcomes of the college experience, nor can a single approach fulfill all planning, policy, or political ends. Successful efforts in assessment, as in anything else, require establishment of carefully drawn and well-understood limits on what can and should be accomplished. The second concept is that of the program. In one form or another, the practice of assessment has been with us since the beginning of the academic enterprise. Indeed, many faculty, in the midst of grading papers, judging class presentations, or evaluating clinical or internship practice, may wonder what all the fuss is about, but such efforts may or may not constitute a program. Institutional assessment programs, as they are emerging, are visible, integrated, ongoing efforts governed by established policy and involving regular (and generally centralized) data collection and analysis. More than a network of resource and technical support for assessment, they serve as structural embodiments of the institution's commitment to self-examination and improvement.

Choices to be made in designing an assessment program are best described in terms of the answers to three basic questions.

1. *Why assess?* This is a question of primary intent, of unit of analysis, and of perspective. What is the program basically for? An answer to this question will determine the fundamental structure of any program, and certain answers will necessary preclude others.

2. *What to assess?* This is a question of explicit content and appropriate level. Among the multitudes of potential outcomes, which are deemed the most important for investigation? An answer to this question will determine which outcomes dimensions receive priority in the evaluation process, regardless of the methods used.

3. *How to assess?* This is a question of method and measurement. In what manner are data actually to be collected, by whom, when, and using what instruments or techniques? Although this is to some extent a technical question, answers must also address feasibility, cost, and the needs of different kinds of users of the resulting information.

These questions must also be addressed in the order given here. Prompted by external pressure, some colleges and universities have attempted quick-fix approaches that rely exclusively on off-the-shelf assessment instruments or that essentially try to duplicate model programs available in the literature. By addressing the "how" question first, most such approaches become quickly enmeshed in political difficulties, because their unclear purposes threaten faculty, or they are ignored, because the information they yield is of no clear use in improving performance. In assessment, as in any other investigation, Kaplan's "Law of the Instrument" is to be avoided: Available methods should not be allowed to dictate the object of inquiry (Kaplan, 1964).

Why to Assess: Determining Intent

Most of the diversity apparent in current approaches to assessment exists because developing programs are designed for quite diverse purposes. Programs described in this volume provide many good illustrations. In comparing their merits, the reader should be aware of their different origins.

In essence, the question of intent is made up of three distinct dimensions. The first concerns the anticipated use of assessment results and recalls the classic distinction between formative and summative evaluation. Some assessment programs are primarily intended to demonstrate or certify achievement. Florida's College-Level Academic Skills Test (CLAST), for example, ensures in principle that each student who enters the upper division has mastered a certain level of reading, writing, and quantitative skills. Although most such approaches apply to individual students, this need not be so. Recent recommendations of the National Governors' Association (1986), for example, call for comparative, aggregated, and publicly available measures of student outcomes in order to judge the performance of individual institutions.

Most emerging assessment approaches (including several state-level initiatives) are intended instead to inform instructional improvement. Most assessment of this kind is undertaken at the program or curricular levels. Item analyses of aggregated student performance on locally designed major field examinations at the University of Tennessee at Knoxville, for example, have led to notable faculty-initiated changes in course content, in curriculum structure, and in teaching approach (Banta, 1985). The widely used ACT College Outcomes Measures Project (COMP) examinations are designed for formative program evaluation, despite comparative scores' public availability. Although not generally seen as outcomes assessment, placement testing of students upon entry into college is also an excellent example of the formative approach. Rather than being used externally to judge or certify student performance, the results of such examinations are generally used in counseling and advisement or to design an individualized program that maximizes each student's chances for success.

Both formative and summative assessment can take place at many levels of analysis, and this possibility constitutes a second dimension of choice. Most assessment programs involve collecting data at one of three possible levels. The programs at Miami–Dade and Ramapo College are good illustrations of student-level approaches. Program-level approaches, in contrast, aggregate student performance across a curriculum or program. Institution-level approaches are similar but aggregate results across the entire institution. Their foundation remains the testing of individual students, but individual records are rarely used or maintained. Indeed, for such instruments as the ACT COMP and for most student survey instruments, individual results have little statistical or substantive meaning. Moreover, because they rely on aggregated data, both program- and institution-level approaches often test or survey only samples of students, rather than requiring all to participate. Assessment programs at Northeast Missouri State University and the University of Tennessee at Knoxville represent combinations of program- and institution-level approaches.

Together, formative-summative and level-of-analysis dimensions determine the basic structure of any institutional assessment program. A final dimension of intent, however, remains: From whose perspective should successful performance be judged? Colleges and universities serve many distinct constituencies, and each institution and constituent group may have a different view of effective performance. The historic assertion of the academy has been that such determinations can be made only by faculty, but political and environmental constraints have caused this view to be received with increasing skepticism. Indeed, much of the accountability movement in higher education can be explained by loss of confidence on the part of state government, potential employers, and the public at large that the academy is capable of determining appropriate performance.

If faculty perspectives are not always useful, what alternatives are available? At least three have become increasingly important. One is that of students themselves. Students approach higher education with a variety of motives, not all of them consistent with the goals we as educational providers intend. Some may approach the enterprise solely from the standpoint of job training, of acquiring the necessary skills to perform effectively in particular professions. With this goal met, they may withdraw fully satisfied. Others may successfully complete programs but not meet their primary goals. Institutions such as community colleges or open-admissions universities that serve heavily part-time clienteles may therefore place considerable evaluative weight on student goal attainment. At such institutions as the Community College of Philadelphia, St. Petersburg Junior College, and Mt. Hood Community College, for example, data on student intent are regularly collected, and the assessment of institutional effectiveness rests to some extent on the degree to which student goals are met.

A second external perspective is provided by employers and other higher education institutions—the primary "consumers" of college graduates. Such clients are satisfied with a given level of performance only if it enables effective performance in the workplace or classroom. Their judgments, both about what is needed and about needed levels of proficiency may differ markedly from those of faculty. The salience of this perspective for any institution will depend, of course, on the degree to which its mission clearly entails service to such constituencies.

A final external perspective, particularly for public colleges and universities, is that of the public at large or, more pointedly, that of their elected representatives. Viewed from this standpoint, higher education is intended to serve identifiable public purposes that may have little direct correspondence with purely academic goals. Among them are ensuring equal access to the presumed benefits of higher education, promoting regional or statewide economic development through the provision of trained manpower, and ensuring minimum levels of functional citizenship among the inhabitants of a state or region.

What to Assess: Determining Outcomes Dimensions

Determining which of many potential outcomes of the undergraduate experience are important can only be an institutional decision, one whose result must be consistent both with the instructional mission the institution defines for itself and with the students it seeks to serve. Certainly, the literature on college outcomes is vast and represents an enormous range of choice (Lenning, 1979; Bowen, 1977; Pace, 1979; Ewell, 1984). Most extant assessment programs, however, tend to examine similar basic dimensions. Among them are the following.

Knowledge Outcomes. Historically, questions of cognitive content have dominated academic discourse, at least at the level of the individual course. Proponents of liberal or general education hold that possession of a common core of concepts and material should be the hallmark of the educated person. Commonly included under this heading are basic knowledge of Western (and occasionally non-Western) civilization, familiarity with key works of literature, or familiarity with important scientific, technical, esthetic, and philosophical principles. Also included are important principles of inquiry associated with key disciplinary groupings. Among these are the principles of (1) experimental inquiry, which rest on verification of propositions through empirical observation; (2) historical or documentary inquiry, which stress verification through comparative or critical evaluation of textual materials; (3) technological inquiry, which emphasize verification of general principles through their concrete application in a problem-solving situation; and (4) esthetic inquiry, which stress the evaluation of truth through key formalistic and interpretive processes.

In addition to imparting general knowledge, typical undergraduate education involves substantial experience in single fields. Therefore, familiarity with the broad history of a particular discipline, knowledge of its current and classic core questions, awareness of its various subfields and targets of inquiry, and knowledge of its available methods and techniques are also included.

Skills Outcomes. In contrast to cognitive content, the skills dimension emphasizes application—not what a student knows, but what he or she actually can do. Oddly, this is a dimension often omitted from the traditional grading process. While performance assessment in clinical or internship settings has become a key aspect of student evaluation in many occupational or professional fields, grading practices in most disciplines continue to emphasize content over application.

For purposes of assessment, skills outcomes can be usefully divided into four areas. The first consists of many basic skills that external critics most often see lacking in college graduates. At the minimum, these include reading comprehension, writing, and computational skills. Because of the external salience of this dimension, basic skills testing is part of several existing or proposed state-mandated assessment programs, among them programs in Florida, Georgia, New Jersey, and Texas.

The second skills area consists of such higher-order cognitive skills as critical thinking, problem solving, and other complex applications of information and learned techniques. Skills of this kind have long been held to be the primary intended outcomes of a liberal arts curriculum. Some observers have considered them also to be products of professional instruction in such fields as law, medicine, and business. Because they are complex, however, available testing instruments are scarce, and such skills are seldom directly assessed outside individual classrooms. Indeed, part of the popularity of the ACT COMP, used by over two hundred institutions, is that it is one of the few widely available instruments that attempt to assess skills of this kind.

Equally important, though seldom explicitly identified as part of college outcomes, is the third area, knowledge-building skills, including skills associated with locating existing knowledge through library catalogues, computer archives, and other sources. Also covered are skills associated with planning and executing independent intellectual projects—for example, problem identification, appropriate use of time, and ability to change direction in the light of new or unavailable evidence. Knowledge building also depends on such technical abilities as familiarity with computers, ability to skim large bodies of written material, and ability to take notes or otherwise record material for later recall.

The fourth area consists of skills required for effective practice in particular occupations or professions. These skills are often tested by certification or licensure examinations and generally include both cognitive recall and simulated application of what has been learned to a complex situation likely to be encountered in practice. Considerable assessment of such skills is already practiced in many professional and occupational programs because individual courses often involve applied or clinical situations.

Attitudes and Values Outcomes. As intended products of college and university instruction, of course, any particular sets of attitudes or values can be controversial. As Pace (1985) has stressed, such individual values as self-esteem and political liberalism are profoundly influenced by the college experience, but it is hard to judge whether they are unambiguously good or bad.

Nevertheless, there are some affective outcomes that all educators believe to be important. Tolerance for diversity and recognition of the value and contributions of other cultures constitute one set. A primary assessment question here is whether the individual can separate his or her evaluation of an argument from its particular cultural context and examine it strictly on its own merits. A second set concerns development of a workable array of personal values that help define identity (Chickering, 1969). Here, emphasis is placed on the structure and integration of personal values and not on their particular content. A third set has to do with social values—for example, taking responsibility for personal action, managing emotion and peer pressure, and having the ability to empathize and compromise appropriately. A final set involves such action-oriented attitudes as persistence, motivation, and task consciousness.

Beyond these four sets, of course, individual institutions may embrace a range of important values. Indeed, for many small, private, liberal arts institutions—particularly those with active religious affiliations—maintaining and developing such values may constitute the heart of the educational enterprise. Investigations of the content or basis of religious belief, or of the development and ability to apply particular ethical principles, are appropriate in such settings and increasingly are being undertaken.

Behavioral Outcomes. Behavior of students and former students is in many respects simply a manifestation of the knowledge, skills, and attitudes developed during college attendance. Nevertheless, most assessment approaches explicitly include what students do during and after attendance as a separate domain of investigation.

While students are enrolled, important elements of their behavior are persistence and program completion, choice of major and persistence within the major field, and course selection and completion. While not strictly outcomes of college attendance, such processes are crucial to assessing a curriculum's impact. Indeed, a major emerging irony of the assessment movement is that by concentrating primarily on documenting outcomes, we have lost sight of the fact that at most of our institutions it is quite rare for two or more of our students undergo the same experience. Documenting this experience should be a key component of any curriculum assessment.

For those no longer enrolled at the institution, both graduates and nongraduates, several kinds of information are commonly collected. They include occupational information, such as employer and current job title, employment history, salary levels, and required skills; further educational history, such as institutions attended, fields studied, persistence or completion of program, and performance while enrolled; professional activities, such as memberships, involvement with professional issues, and recognized contributions to the profession; and contributions to community and society, such as voluntary membership and participation, voting, and political participation.

Together, these four basic assessment dimensions provide a considerable "menu" for institutional choice. No institution can hope to assess them all, although there are few that most of us could agree to discard as unimportant; yet we must choose if we are to build workable programs. The key point in making choices is to recall that colleges and universities have quite diverse missions and instructional goals. Careful analysis of these expressed intentions, and clear identification of their implied priorities, are generally prerequisites to choosing what will be assessed. Without such attention, the natural tendency is to allow available methods to determine the shape of the program.

How to Assess: Determining the Best Approach

Despite recent claims to the contrary, researchers have developed many instruments and techniques for assessing the outcomes of college (Pace, 1979). Admittedly, the vast majority of instruments were designed for other purposes than curricular assessment or accountability, but we are certainly not starting from scratch. Indeed, five quite different methodological traditions are currently being tapped by the assessment movement: standardized cognitive tests originally designed for student selection and placement; locally developed comprehensive examinations devised by individual faculties to demonstrate mastery of particular curricula; face-to-face interview and task-performance techniques similar to those used in business and professional communities to ascertain and develop individual potentials; survey questionnaires of students, former students, employers and other key constituents, and community residents; and traditional institutional research studies of student persistence, program completion, and enrollment behavior.

Each methodological "family" can produce evidence about a number of outcomes dimensions (Harris, 1985). Each, however, also has important strengths and weaknesses, both substantive and logistical. Each approach is briefly presented here, with a discussion of its strengths and weaknesses.

Standardized Testing. Certainly, the most frequently posed image of assessment involves large numbers of students completing computer-scored multiple-choice examinations. Many institutional programs do rely heavily on administering standardized cognitive achievement tests. Most of the time, however, these tests have been designed for other purposes. Popular alternatives for assessing general knowledge and skills, for example, include the ACT assessment designed for purposes of college admissions, the College-Level Examination Program (CLEP) offered by Educational Testing Service (ETS) for use in awarding credit by examination, the Graduate Record Examination (GRE) offered by ETS for graduate school admission, and the Pre-Professional Skills Test (PPST) designed to assess readiness for professional practice. Occasionally these are administered at several points in a student's academic career in order to determine the gain due to instruction. Often they are administered on a sample basis, rather than being required for all students.

Popular alternatives for assessing knowledge and skills in individual major programs also rely heavily on existing instruments designed for other purposes. These include the GRE field examinations, CLEP subject examinations, a host of professional certification examinations (for example, the National League of Nursing Examination and the National CPA Examination), and a number of preprofessional assessment instruments for particular fields (for example, the National Teachers Examination, the Medical College Admissions Test, the Law School Admissions Test, and the Graduate Management Admissions Test).

More recently, standardized instruments have been developed especially for large-scale assessment. State-sponsored tests of basic skills, such as the CLAST, the New Jersey Basic Skills Test, and the Georgia Regents Examination, are good examples. Instruments that attempt to assess both knowledge and skills dimensions of general education, such as the ACT COMP, are also emerging. As yet, however, standardized instruments designed to assess higher-order skills are rare.

There are many arguments for using standardized achievement tests to assess knowledge and skills. First, they are relatively easy to administer and, although costly if used in volume, they do not entail large investments of faculty time. Second, established standardized tests are generally less open to charges of subjectivity than are other methods. Third, because standardized tests are administered at many institutions, it is possible to compare scores among institutions. This is attractive for accountability purposes, but it can also be an advantage in local curriculum improvement, provided that parallel results from appropriate peer institutions can be obtained.

Standardized tests can also involve substantial disadvantages. First, their coverage may or may not reflect the content of a particular institution's curriculum or program. GRE field examinations in political science, for example, cover different branches of the discipline in varying proportions, and these emphases may or may not represent the institution's own approach to the discipline. In such examinations as the ACT COMP, moreover, it may be difficult to identify any particular portion of the curriculum that is directly linked to test performance. Second, the results of standardized examinations are generally reported as a single performance score, or at most as four to six subscores. This practice provides faculty with very little to go on in identifying which portions of a curriculum are working and which are not. Until now, few testing organizations have been willing to release "item scores," or the performance of students on individual examination questions, although most organizations are under increasing pressure to do so. Third, normative comparison scores on standardized tests may be inappropriate for general curriculum evaluation. On the GRE, for example, norms are compiled on the basis of those who took the test—in this case, graduate school–bound seniors nationwide. This pool may or may not be appropriate for comparison with a given institution's entire graduating class.

Locally Designed Examinations. Comprehensive general examinations were once a familiar part of most undergraduate curricula. Their intent was to evaluate student ability to integrate and apply knowledge and skills gained throughout a curriculum or program but not specific to individual courses. Recently, pressures for enhanced assessment have stimulated colleges and universities to reexamine the senior comprehensive—in general education or, more commonly, in the major field—as an alternative to standardized testing.

The traditional senior comprehensive examination was an integral part of the curriculum. It generally entailed objective demonstration of a student's mastery of core concepts and material. More important, it involved application of these concepts to an extensive critical essay or problem-solving exercise. Furthermore, students were expected to pass the comprehensive as a condition of graduation. The primary intent of the test was to determine what students knew and not to identify the strengths and weaknesses of the curriculum.

Locally designed tests that are intended primarily to provide evidence for program improvement are of more recent vintage. Often, as illustrated by many of the University of Tennessee at Knoxville's major field examinations, they arise out of the necessity to build local assessments in the absence of available standardized alternatives. Occasionally, as illustrated by an experimental sophomore-junior project at King's College (Wilkes-Barre, Pennsylvania) or a locally designed test of general education (termed *Form C*) at Olivet Nazarene College, they arise out of dissatisfaction with the match in content and coverage between available standardized tests and the curriculum. Locally designed curriculum assessments such as these are relatively infrequent at present. They are strongly emerging as a preferred approach, however, as evidenced by the plans of state-wide "pilot" institutions, such as Kean College in New Jersey, James Madison University in Virginia, and SUNY-Plattsburgh.

Major advantages of locally designed cognitive instruments counter the primary deficiencies of standardized examinations. First, they can be tailored to an individual curriculum, reflecting both its particular areas of emphasis and its distinctive style of presentation. Second, analyses of results can be undertaken in considerable detail. For example, item analyses can reveal precisely the areas where students performed well or badly. Third, modes of student response other than multiple-choice formats can be used—for example, essays or task- and problem-solving exercises. Although difficult to score comparatively, they present less of a disadvantage in local settings. Most important, perhaps, because they are designed by faculty, examinations of this kind are seen as legitimate by those most involved in the curriculum. Consequently, their results are much more likely to be used in making improvements (Banta, 1985).

Major drawbacks also complement those of standardized tests. Because they are designed by interested parties and reflect only the priorities of particular departments or institutions, local assessments may be less externally credible than stadardized alternatives. Moreover, comparison information from other institutions or programs is by definition unavailable. (As local assessments become more common, however, this drawback may decline. For example, a number of departments in Tennessee colleges and universities have recently cooperated to develop major field examinations in common.) Finally, local assessments can be costly to produce, particularly in scarce faculty time. Furthermore, most faculty lack the training or experience to build good tests. For these reasons, institutions committed to this approach provide support in the form of funds for faculty and direct technical assistance in test construction and evaluation.

Individualized Assessment. Another established assessment tradition uses intensive, individually tailored methods to identify the strengths and weaknesses of each student. Using a variety of interview-based techniques, task exercises, and specialized assessment instruments, approaches of this kind have become prominent tools for "human resource development" in business corporations. In higher education, such techniques have long held a place in some professional graduate programs, particularly in business and law. With the prominent exception of Alverno College (Milwaukee), however, similar techniques have not been practiced in traditional academic disciplines, nor have they been applied to undergraduate curricula (Alverno College Faculty, 1985).

Assessment in this tradition uses a variety of techniques and may involve simultaneous investigation of knowledge, skills, and values. For example, in addition to open-ended interviews, students at Alverno may complete one or more exercises designed to tap critical thinking ability by use of the Perry scheme. They may also engage in a moral choice exercise using Kohlberg's scale and may complete a variety of psychological personality inventories (Mentkowski and Loacker, 1985). Evidence from all these sources is integrated by a trained assessor for inclusion in individual student portfolios. To address more specific, job-related skills and attitudes, simulated task performances are often used. Students must identify and solve typical problems in case settings, with their responses directly observed by assessors or provided by means of essays or debriefing interviews. This approach has proved particularly suitable for such fields as nursing, where clinical practice and classroom instruction go hand in hand.

Such approaches, of course, represent a definition of assessment that stresses its formative nature and concentrates on developing the individual, rather than the program or the institution. As a result, their strengths include direct benefits to teaching and learning, greater integration of a usually diverse curriculum, and considerable faculty involvement. Indeed, at a place like Alverno, assessment and teaching are virtually synonymous. A major payoff of an assessment center approach, moreover, is multiple evaluation of student performance. Many instruments and techniques are used in the process, and many individual assessors are involved. As a result, unlike traditional course grading, the evaluation process is considerably less vulnerable to charges of subjectivity. Finally, assessment can be directly linked to intended skills through complex simulations of multifaceted problems or professional situations.

At the same time, individualized assessment has considerable drawbacks. First, its intensity may demand virtual reconstruction of the curriculum—probably a valuable exercise at most institutions but not one to be undertaken lightly. Although cost is difficult to determine in such situations, because assessment is an integral part of teaching, initial investments certainly will be high. Furthermore, assessments of this kind do not provide much summative information suitable for communicating to outside audiences. Here, Alverno's approach is to supplement internal assessment with more formal validation studies, using recognized instruments or directly involving such external constituencies as members of local business or professional communities.

Survey Questionnaire Approaches. Student surveys are among the most established and available of approaches to outcomes data collection. Types of surveys in common use, designed by testing and research organizations or by institutions themselves, include studies of entering students, currently enrolled students, and former students (graduates and nongraduates). Useful information about student outcomes can also be obtained from surveys that elicit the reactions of faculty, employers, and citizens in an institution's service region.

While questionnaires are most appropriate for collecting information on attitudes and values or for documenting students' career and educational development, they may also be used to obtain self-reports of knowledge gains, changes in skill levels, and students' level of involvement in the learning process. Although better methods are potentially available in each of the latter areas, questionnaires are an extremely efficient method for gathering some information on these dimensions. For example, innovative surveys intended to tap such complex concepts as Chickering's "vectors of identity" or Perry's "levels of critical thinking" have been undertaken at Texas A. & M. and are currently being replicated at James Madison University (Erwin, 1983).

Surveys of entering students (for example, the national Cooperative Institutional Research Program study administered each year by UCLA) generally include student goals and aspirations, perceived deficiencies in basic skills areas, intended major, and high school background. Surveys of currently enrolled students (for example, the ACT Evaluation Survey Service or the National Center for Higher Education Management Systems (NCHEMS)/College Board Student Outcomes Information Service) include progress toward achieving individual goals, perceived development of cognitive skills, current attitudes and satisfaction, and reactions to various aspects of the institutional environment. Instruments such as Pace's College Student Experiences Questionnaire (CSEQ) also include particularly useful self-reports of student investment in the learning process—for example, utilization of various campus resources and facilities. For former students (graduates and nongraduates), these questions are generally supplemented by items concerning current employment situation and history, subsequent enrollment and performance at other colleges and universities, and perceived relationship between education or training received and current job or educational situation.

There are several benefits of questionnaire-based assessment approaches. First, compared to testing or interview-based assessments, surveys are relatively cheap. Most cost from two to four dollars per respondent, including administration and analysis, compared to at least three times this cost for most cognitive tests (Ewell and Jones, 1985). Second, surveys are extremely flexible. The same instrument can be used to gather some kinds of information on a large number of quite different outcomes dimensions. Third, surveys may be virtually the only way to assess some attitudinal outcomes and may be one of the few available methods for obtaining information on graduates. Finally, survey information has considerable external face validity. For most external audiences, it is hard to argue with the testimony of a satisfied customer.

Despite their flexibility and efficiency, survey approaches have many drawbacks. Most important, they are only indirect indicators of knowledge and skills. Because growth in these two areas is self-reported, survey results are considered less credible than more objective assessments. More important, meaningful standards of attainment are virtually impossible to establish. As a result, institutions often use surveys as less costly supplements to sample-based cognitive achievement tests. A second drawback to questionnaire studies is potential lack of response. Because most surveys are mailed, response rates of 30 percent or lower are not uncommon. Unless better response rates can be obtained (and, indeed, most institutions that persist have found that they can be), the results of such studies are bound to be suspect. Finally, because they are broad and flexible, most student surveys are relatively imprecise. Although they may signal the presence of a curricular or an environmental problem, further investigation is generally required to determine precisely what is wrong and what to do about it.

Tracking Student Behavior. At all institutions, considerable information on student behavior is already available. Unfortunately, most record systems are not maintained in formats suitable for tracking student performance over time in order to determine patterns of enrollment and persistence. In the last decade, stimulated by a need for accurate studies of student retention so as to project and manage enrollment, institutional researchers have developed a number of sound approaches for undertaking such studies (Terenzini, 1987; Ewell, 1987). Most involve constructing a number of student cohort groups, whose enrollment patterns and levels of performance are followed in detail over a given period. Typically, the kinds of behavior examined include term-to-term persistence, program completion and time to completion, course passage rates, and grade point performance. Such systems occasionally track actual patterns of course taking, progress toward the attainment of previously established educational goals, and remediation of academic deficiencies. In addition, they may include information drawn from periodically administered student questionnaires or cognitive tests. Information on enrollment behavior, of course, is not, strictly speaking outcomes information, and this limitation constitutes its primary drawback. Nevertheless, enrollment data can be extremely useful in interpreting test scores, survey responses, and other "true" outcomes data by documenting what the actual enrollment experience of each student has been.

Each of these five methodological "families" has something to contribute to an outcomes assessment program. Moreover, some approaches are more suitable for assessing particular outcomes dimensions or are especially appropriate for a given audience. Because of the general imprecision of educational measurement, however, institutions are well advised to invest in more than one method.

Implementing an Assessment Program: Concluding Comments

The foregoing discussion outlines a "menu" for institutional choice; it by no means provides guidance on how to proceed. Readers are left to examine the rest of this volume for concrete illustrations of how appropriate choices are enacted. Nevertheless, emerging experience in implementing campus-based assessment programs suggests the following practical guidelines.

1. *Capitalize on existing information.* Most colleges and universities

collect far more information on student outcomes than they think they do. Registrars' offices, testing centers, placement offices, counseling centers, and individual academic departments are all good places to look for existing information. Carefully compiling diverse information to reveal a composite picture of student experience is a good first step toward implementing assessment.

2. *Create a visible center for assessment activity.* Assessment makes a powerful statement about an institution's concern for the development of its students. This statement must be organizationally visible. At the same time, smooth implementation demands coordination and control. Therefore, most successful assessment programs designate a particular office or staff-supported faculty committee for housing and directing assessment activity across the campus, fund it adequately, and provide it with powerful channels for disseminating results.

3. *Experiment with pilot programs.* On any campus, assessment is a novel and controversial endeavor. Faculty will be apprehensive, administrators defensive, and students indifferent. Moreover, untried methods will be proposed, the consequences of which are unclear. Beginning with a series of varied pilot programs, using volunteer units and departments, allows a number of methods to be explored simultaneously. Furthermore, faculty in successful pilot departments can serve as powerful advocates for assessment across the campus.

4. *Discover and critically evaluate existing model programs.* One advantage of beginning an assessment program now is that many of the basic mistakes have already been made. The best institutional efforts began with a year or two of careful study—examining a variety of tools, instruments, techniques, and administrative arrangements—before proposal of individual approaches.

5. *Use the results in identifiable ways.* Assessment will not be taken seriously on or off campus if its results are not taken seriously. If a periodic report is all that is produced, and if assessment results do not show up visibly in decisions about curriculum, academic policy, and budget, then the process will have failed.

Determining an appropriate assessment approach is an art that depends on clear knowledge of what is intended, solid research about available instruments and about the experiences of other institutions, and accurate diagnosis of the local organizational and political climate. As in any other art, there is no best way, but there are many ways of going wrong. The cases illustrated in this volume should help you avoid mistakes.

References

Alverno College Faculty. *Assessment at Alverno College.* Milwaukee, Wis.: Alverno Productions, 1985.

24

Banta, T. W. (ed.). *Performance Funding in Higher Education: A Case Study.* Boulder, Colo.: National Center for Higher Education Management Systems (NCHEMS), 1985.

Bowen, H. R. *Investment in Learning: The Individual and Social Value of American Higher Education.* San Francisco: Jossey-Bass, 1977.

Chickering, A. W. *Education and Identity.* San Francisco: Jossey-Bass, 1969.

Erwin, T. D. "The Scale of Intellectual Development: Measuring Perry's Scheme." *Journal of College Student Personnel*, January, 1983, pp. 6–11.

Ewell, P. T. *The Self-Regarding Institution: Information for Excellence.* Boulder, Colo.: National Center for Higher Education Management Systems (NCHEMS), 1984.

Ewell, P. T. "Principles of Longitudinal Enrollment Analysis: Conducting Retention and Student Flow Studies." In J. A. Muffo and G. W. McLaughlin (eds.), *A Primer on Institutional Research.* Tallahassee, Fla.: Association for Institutional Research, 1987.

Ewell, P. T., and Jones, D. P. "The Costs of Assessment." In C. P. Adelman (ed.), *Assessment in American Higher Education: Issues and Contexts.* Washington, D.C.: Office of Educational Research and Improvement, U.S. Department of Education, 1985.

Harris, J. "Assessing Outcomes in Higher Education." In C. P. Adelman (ed.), *Assessment in American Higher Education: Issues and Contexts.* Washington, D.C.: Office of Educational Research and Improvement, U.S. Department of Education, 1985.

Kaplan, A. W. *The Logic of Inquiry.* San Francisco: Chandler, 1964.

Lenning, O. W. *Previous Attempts to Structure Educational Outcomes and Outcome-Related Concepts.* Boulder, Colo.: National Center for Higher Education Management Systems (NCHEMS), 1979.

Mentkowski, M., and Loacker, G. "Assessing and Validating the Outcomes of College." In P. T. Ewell (ed.), *Assessing Educational Outcomes.* New Directions for Institutional Research, no. 47. San Francisco: Jossey-Bass, 1985.

National Governors' Association. *Time for Results: The Governors' 1991 Report on Education.* Washington, D.C.: The National Governors' Association Center for Policy Research and Analysis, 1986.

Pace, C. R. *Measuring Outcomes of College: Fifty Years of Findings and Recommendations for the Future.* San Francisco: Jossey-Bass, 1979.

Pace, C. R. "Perspectives and Problems in Student Outcomes Research." In P. T. Ewell (ed.), *Assessing Educational Outcomes.* New Directions for Institutional Research, no. 47. San Francisco, Jossey-Bass, 1985.

Terenzini, P. T. "Studying Student Retention and Attrition." In J. A. Muffo and G. W. McLaughlin (eds.), *A Primer on Institutional Research.* Tallahassee, Fla.: Association for Institutional Research, 1987.

Peter T. Ewell is senior associate at the National Center for Higher Management Systems (NCHEMS).

When a state seeks to improve the quality of higher education through mandatory assessment of student learning, it is necessary to examine existing quality-assurance mechanisms and to consider the utility of models providing more comprehensive data.

A State University Perspective on Student Outcomes Assessment

William E. Vandament

The sudden emergence of state governments' interest in assessment programs prompts some questions. Why have the traditional measures of institutional validation suddenly become inadequate? How, in the face of positive accreditation reports, evidence of faculty quality, and growth in enrollments and rates of degree productivity, can we ask whether students are learning anything in college?

Given the doubts raised by the test scores of college graduates, increases in the amount of remedial instruction on college campuses, declining average scores on the GRE, complaints from business and industry about deficiencies in basic communication and computational skills of college graduates, and the highly publicized critical reports compiled by various commissions, it is easy to understand the wish of elected public officials to make sure taxpayers' money is not being misspent.

The political appeal of an approach promising to provide quantifiable evidence of gains in student achievement for each public college or university is self-evident, particularly in times of increased competition for tax dollars. Indeed, the National Governors' Association (1986) recommended that state governments require public colleges and universities to

D. F. Halpern (ed.). *Student Outcomes Assessment: What Institutions Stand to Gain.*
New Directions for Higher Education, no. 59. San Francisco: Jossey-Bass, Fall 1987.

implement systematic, comparable programs to measure undergraduate student learning. It further recommended that state funding formulas for public colleges and universities be adjusted in such a way that information gained from assessments could be linked to institutional efforts directed at improving undergraduate learning.

While concurring with the need for state governments to develop better means to monitor the effectiveness of their systems of higher education, the Education Commission of the States (1986) urged states "not to develop a single assessment instrument to be implemented uniformly at all institutions, or even across institutions with similar missions." Aware of the complexities involved in attempting to evaluate the quality of educational outcomes for groups of students or for single institutions (let alone multicampus systems), and mindful of the internecine competition for funding that such a policy would unleash, the commission's report recommends (p. 32), "Assessment should not be an end in itself. Rather, it should be an integral part of an institution's strategy to improve teaching and learning and of the state's strategy to monitor the effectiveness of its system of higher education."

The divergent views set forth in the reports of these two groups—the former exclusively and the latter in large part composed of state governors—define the axis of public debate on institutional assessment. Systematic collection of data about students' knowledge, skills, and attitudes at key points in the undergraduate experience is perceived by both groups as a powerful tool for improving higher education. Both groups recommend assessment programs as a matter of state policy, but fundamental and far-reaching differences exist in their conceptions of assessment and the ways in which it can best be applied.

A critical issue for the California State University (CSU) is what forms comprehensive assessment should take and who should devise them. University leaders have raised persuasive objections to evaluating the highly individual and complex outcomes of undergraduate experience on the basis of students' performance on nationally normed, standardized tests. Such measures would yield data that would be as inconclusive as grade point averages, and the use of these measures would have the effect of forcing curricula into narrow bands of demonstrable outcomes. Recourse to standardized tests would undermine commitment both to developing the higher-order critical, creative, and ethical sensibilities that distinguish the truly educated from the adequately trained and to developing goals of increased participation and degree-completion rates among underrepresented minorities.

Acknowledging the danger of reliance on standardized test scores should not dissuade us from looking at the benefits that appropriate assessment programs might offer. In fact, CSU already employs comprehensive assessment instruments. The English Placement and Elementary-Level

Mathematics Tests are faculty-developed, institutionally approved, and nationally recognized examples of entry-level testing used as a tool to improve learning. The CSU graduation writing assessment requirement, on most campusess a test, was adopted to ensure attainment of upper-division writing skills as a prerequisite for the baccalaureate degree.

CSU academic departments also make extensive use of externally developed comprehensive examinations. GRE or licensure exam results of graduates pursuing postbaccalaureate degrees are routinely reported in formal, periodic program reviews. Many departments monitor comprehensive achievements of majors in capstone courses or senior projects. Alumni and currently enrolled students are periodically surveyed regarding their perceptions about their majors.

Improvement in these instruments or in their systematic employment may be needed, of course, but few would seriously argue that these data have no value in indicating how well a department prepares its students. Most would agree, I suspect, that these tests are inadequate for making judgments about the overall effectiveness of academic programs or the quality of students' experience on campus.

From the CSU perspective, then, the state legislature's interest in assessment models suggests that we need to take what we are already doing a step further: to devise means, sufficient in number and sophistication, to provide an adequate base of information linking students' evolving abilities to specific components of our academic programs and of the institutional setting. In short, we are being challenged to apply, collectively and publicly, the discipline inherent in our scholarly activities to the shaping and assessment of the undergraduate experience.

The history of other universities that have attempted to do this is instructive and encouraging. Measuring how well the institutional goals are being realized in students' experience requires precise clarification of expectations and creation or adoption of appropriate instruments. This process, in turn, has often had the effect of redirecting faculty energy, otherwise devoted to highly individualized scholarly pursuits, to institutional programs and their consequences for students.

Colleges and universities that have developed successful assessment programs report several positive gains for faculty: renewed enthusiasm for teaching, revitalization of interest in students' educational growth and in learning across the disciplines, and newfound pleasure in working with colleagues from one's own and other departments and schools. Faculty development, in its most rewarding sense, has been the principal payoff for universities that have wrestled with this challenge.

To sum up my own CSU perspective on student outcomes assessment, I understand the reasons for the interest of our elected representatives in developing better tools to evaluate what California taxpayers are getting in return for their huge annual investment in public postsecondary educa-

28

tion. I also recognize that the imposition of reductive, standardized measures of student performance is inconsistent with the diversity of institutional goals and settings in the state and may pit the systems, and the campuses of each system, against one another in destructive competition for resources. I encourage campuses to examine carefully the various approaches to assessing student outcomes. They have the potential of helping us do better what we are already trying to accomplish.

References

Education Commission of the States. *Transforming the State Role in Undergraduate Education: Time for a Different View*. Denver: Colo.: Working Party on Effective State Action to Improve Undergraduate Education, Education Commission of the States, 1986.
National Governors' Association. *Time for Results: The Governors' 1991 Report on Education*. Washington, D.C.: The National Governors' Association Center for Policy Research and Analysis, 1986.

William E. Vandament is provost and vice-chancellor of academic affairs at the California State University Office of the Chancellor, Long Beach, California.

Changing demographics, public expectations, and economic circumstances mean that traditional measures of postsecondary educational quality—inputs to the system—may need to be supplemented.

Outcomes Assessment in the California Master Plan

Lee Kerschner

Clearly, quality control is a theme underlying virtually any discussion of public policy. In the case of education, a significant portion of state and federal budgets, and hence of the taxpayer's dollar, is given over to public education. The public demand for quality in return for dollars spent has never been more evident than in recent years, beginning with the K–12 reform movement. The groundswell of demand for better programs, better teachers, and better results has extended into postsecondary education, and the California Commission for the Review of the Master Plan for Higher Education is looking at options for responding to that groundswell.

We in higher education traditionally have measured our own success and the quality of our programs by inputs to the system. In other words, we look at the academic and extracurricular achievements of entering students, the achievements and qualifications of our faculty, the size of our libraries, and the quality of our instructional materials. These help foster success and are worthwhile measures that should not be entirely forsaken; but social, economic, and demographic forecasts for the future indicate that these measures alone may not be sufficient as complete measures of quality.

In the near future, the potential student pool will be more widely varied in age and ethnicity, and our usual measures of student quality—

D. F. Halpern (ed.). *Student Outcomes Assessment: What Institutions Stand to Gain.*
New Directions for Higher Education, no. 59. San Francisco: Jossey-Bass, Fall 1987.

high school grade point averages and test scores—may be far less meaningful than they are now. A crucial shortage of faculty will demand greater institutional flexibility and creativity in supplying teachers. Therefore, our usual measures of faculty quality—academic credentials, research prowess, and publishing history—may also be far less meaningful. Increasing competition for limited funds, as well as the demand for new information technologies, will pose new challenges to the development of instructional materials. Our usual measures of quality in this area as well—the size of libraries and the numbers and variety of books available—will likewise be far less meaningful.

One measure of quality that could be added to a formula for the future is student outcomes assessment. Theoretically, if we can look at what goes into the system and say that it is good, and then if we can look at what comes out and say that it is also good, we ought to be comfortable with what is going on inside the system. I say "theoretically" because student outcomes assessment is not a simple matter; rather, it is rife with a whole series of public policy questions that must be answered before outcomes data can be used appropriately.

An immediate question that comes to mind is "What should we be assessing?" I refer to what I call the Robins in the Spring fallacy. My brother taught in Nigeria in the mid 1960s, in the former British schools. One of his biggest frustrations was that the whole curriculum was focused on the British entrance exams, so that a student would leave school with the ability to pass those exams. My brother had to make sure that these Nigerian students knew that robins come in the spring, even though in Nigeria there are no robins and no spring. To state the obvious, teaching toward this particular goal had absolutely no relevance to the circumstances, yet there it was: a goal that had to be met for its own sake. In moving toward institutionalizing some sort of student outcomes assessment, we run the risk of assessing for the sake of assessment unless we clearly identify what we are looking for.

Another question is "To what end shall we conduct assessments?" One obvious answer would be to ensure that the state is spending its money wisely in public postsecondary education, but there are other possible answers. For instance, shall we attempt to make the institutions accountable to the state, rather than to the high ideals of research and education in the various disciplines? Shall we attempt to quantify any qualitative change that has taken place among students? Or shall we attempt to set our institutions along the path of always trying to better the previous year's measurements in order to prove they are continually improving? Again, to avoid assessment for its own sake, it will be important to identify why we want to know the results of assessment.

Of course, all of this assumes that student outcomes assessment is appropriate, an assumption I would not ask the California Commission to accept without first considering some opposing views. For example, Boyer (1986) has eloquently expressed concern that, of the Western countries, we have the most tested, assessed, and measured student body. In Germany, you come in the classroom door, you sign up, you take a test. At the end of the year, you come back and take another test. If you pass, both you and the institution are deemed successful, but this system has little to do with program quality. There is little focus in Germany on whether students come to class, actively participate in the learning process, or actually gain anything permanent from the experience. Is not the discipline of going to school, writing papers, engaging in open discussion, and doing all the other things that go beyond "just the facts" part of what we want our students to come away with? Boyer says outcomes assessment could well be a rather simplistic answer to a set of very complicated problems, and the California Commission will need to come to grips with that possibility before it can, in good conscience, recommend any kind of regular program for outcomes assessment.

Nationally, the conventional wisdom is that undergraduate education is one of the major problems in higher education today. Several national reports agree that undergraduate education is fundamentally fragmented and lacks clear goals. As a nation, we have focused on what we want to accomplish through higher education at the undergraduate level. It seems to me that this is an obvious prerequisite to institutionalizing student outcomes assessment as any kind of measure.

Reference

Boyer, E. Untitled address presented at the 69th annual meeting of the American Council on Education, San Francisco, October 1986.

Lee Kerschner is the executive director of the California Master Plan for Higher Education.

Part 2.
Four Models of
Student Outcomes Assessment

Student outcomes assessment programs are not all alike. The type of program designed—including what gets measured, how, and when—is determined by purpose and intended use of the data collected. In Part 2, four very different assessment programs are described, along with rationales for the types of instruments adopted and the ways the data are being used to improve curricular offerings and student support services. Involvement of and impact on all members of the college community (students, faculty, administrators, support staff) vary among the four models. Florida's rising junior exam typifies a "gateway" approach to assessment. Trenton State College in New Jersey has concentrated its assessment efforts on the general education portion of the curriculum. In contrast, Northeast Missouri State University has opted to assess learner gains in academic majors. The University of Tennessee adopted its model in response to a legislative initiative that provides additional funding (beyond the baseline generated by usual formulas) for state universities that can document excellence in several predetermined areas.

Comparisons among these four types of programs reveal the multifaceted nature of assessing student outcomes and should provide a background for making the numerous decisions that are part of planning and implementing a comprehensive program of assessment.

Assessment information must be integrated and interpreted, disseminated widely, considered by decision makers, and used to improve programs.

Performance Funding in Tennessee: Stimulus for Program Improvement

Trudy W. Banta, Marian S. Moffett

The Assessment Coordinator's Perspective

Since human behavior is shaped by expectations, a procedure initiated by individuals who anticipate negative consequences may well yield negative results. Conversely, positive expectations of a procedure may assist in producing positive outcomes, even though the procedure may be difficult. If the faculty approaches assessment by asking what it may contribute to a program or an institution, the assessment process may provide information that will increase the efficiency of decision makers.

Over the past five years, we at the University of Tennessee at Knoxville (UTK) have undertaken a comprehensive assessment program. We do not consider our program a model for any other; every faculty must have its own objectives for assessment. We do have five years of experience with a comprehensive program, however, and some of that experience may be helpful. Objectives can provide direction for instructors and students alike. Lectures and class discussions, out-of-class assignments, and tests questions should be linked to course objectives. Students should be informed of their progress in meeting objectives. Test performance and students' per-

D. F. Halpern (ed.). *Student Outcomes Assessment: What Institutions Stand to Gain.*
New Directions for Higher Education, no. 59. San Francisco: Jossey-Bass, Fall 1987.

36

ceptions of the quality of courses can be used to assess the overall effectiveness of courses and, ultimately, of the educational program to which the courses belong.

External and Internal Motivators

The external forces that are impelling faculty and administrators to consider assessment can be placed into four categories: state initiatives, accreditation standards, national reports, and funded projects.

State Initiatives. Public policy initiatives vary in their intrusiveness—for example, Florida's mandatory testing program for rising juniors, the performance funding initiatives in Tennessee, and the challenge grants for pilot projects offered in Virginia and New Jersey. State-mandated examinations for students do not encourage institutions to develop their own assessment activities. In Tennessee, the types of tests to be used by institutions are not specified, but since a number of assessment activities are (Banta, 1986), the Tennessee program stands between the one in Florida and those in Virginia and New Jersey in terms of its prescriptive nature. Funds for excellence, in Virginia, and challenge grants, in New Jersey, have been made available for institutions to finance the development of assessment programs responsive to their own objectives and needs.

Accreditation Standards. In recent years, all six of the nation's regional accrediting associations for higher education have adopted criteria related to the assessment of outcomes. The Southern Association of Colleges and Schools has assumed leadership among the regional associations in implementing its "institutional effectiveness" criterion. From 1986 on, all institutions of higher education in the Southeast will be expected to provide evidence that faculty and administrators have established a clear purpose for education within the institution, formulated educational goals consistent with that purpose, evaluated the achievement of those goals in a variety of ways, and used the results of evaluation to improve institutional effectiveness (Southern Association of Colleges and Schools, 1984).

National Reports. Involvement in Learning (Study Group on the Conditions of Excellence in American Higher Education, 1984) was the first of several national reports containing strong recommendations that institutions of higher education undertake efforts to assess student outcomes. The three principal recommendations of this report directed institutions to (1) formulate objectives for student development and use them to make explicit to students what the institution expects of them, (2) increase students' involvement in their education, and (3) assess student progress in attaining the institution's objectives.

The Association of American Colleges (1985) issued a report with a chapter on assessment that contained this statement: "The colleges themselves must be held responsible for developing evaluations that the public can respect" (p. 33). The National Governors' Association (1986) produced a report that included a recommendation for institutions of higher education to "invest significant time and resources" in assessment (p. 159). Taken together, these reports communicate a clear message to colleges and universities: Assessment of educational outcomes has become an issue of high priority for those within and outside academe who have an interest in improving the quality of higher education.

Funded Projects. The Kellogg Foundation and the U.S. Department of Education's Fund for the Improvement of Postsecondary Education (FIPSE) have provided money to support assessment initiatives at a number of institutions. UTK used a Kellogg grant in 1982 to study the potential impact on the institution of the state's performance funding program. In 1986, UTK was awarded a FIPSE grant to establish the national Assessment Resource Center.

Institutional Benefits

In addition to the external factors motivating institutions to look at assessment, we should consider a number of internal benefits that can be derived from an assessment program. Alverno College and Northeast Missouri State University are the pioneers in assessment. In the 1970s, leaders at those institutions had the vision to see what might be gained from undertaking comprehensive assessment programs. Those of us who have come more recently to this arena have discovered that institutions can use assessment to demonstrate their accountability to the constituencies they serve, provide direction for improving programs and services, supplement strategic planning processes, develop strategies for improving student retention, establish comparative advantage vis-à-vis other institutions, suggest the content for faculty development programs, stimulate curriculum reform, and even enhance campus fundraising activities.

Purposes of Assessment at UTK

When it became clear in 1981 that the Tennessee Higher Education Commission (THEC) actually meant to begin basing a portion of higher education funding on performance criteria, there was considerable consternation among administrators at UTK, who viewed the THEC action as a potential violation of academic freedom. One of the authors of this chapter was serving as an administrative intern in the Office of the Chancellor at that time, and her experience in directing program evaluations for public schools gave her a perspective from which to view the THEC proposal as a stimulus for undertaking comprehensive program evaluation in higher education. With the assistance of a small grant obtained from the Kellogg Foundation, we established three task forces at UTK, composed of faculty and administrators who would study the implications of an instructional evaluation program that would include assessments of student achievement in general education, assessments of student achievement in major fields, and ways to measure perceptions of program quality on the part of enrolled students, alumni, nonreturning students, and others.

The three Kellogg task forces concluded after six months that a comprehensive assessment program should be undertaken at UTK to establish the status of our programs in meeting their objectives for student development, to provide direction for improving and strengthening these programs, and to improve the quality of information used in making decisions about relative priorities for program enhancement and for allocation of internal resources.

More specifically, the task force members recommended that the university use the outcome information to develop the institution's mission statement and related planning documents, to conduct comprehensive academic program reviews, and to evaluate the university's status in achieving its planning goals.

In 1985, the one-paragraph UTK statement of mission was revised to include the following sentence: "The university's high standards are enforced through a rigorous system of program review and assessment." The guidelines for the self-study that provide direction for UTK's comprehensive review process were expanded to include a section on program outcomes. In addition to describing its resources in the self-study (credentials of faculty; abilities of incoming students; level of financing; adequacy of facilities, equipment, and library resources), each unit is now encouraged to report on the achievement of its students in general education and in the major fields, and to report on the results of opinion surveys administered to students, alumni, dropouts, and employers concerning program quality. Other outcome measures suggested in the guidelines include rates of job placement, rates and quality of placement in graduate or professional education, and examples of external recognition accorded students and alumni. Thus, data on outcomes are considered by reviewers as they assess how a program is meeting objectives for student development and as they make recommendations for program improvement. In turn, reviewers' recommendations are used to influence administrative decisions concerning priorities for improvement and resource allocation.

Assessment Procedures

There are several assessment procedures that our Kellogg task forces have deemed appropriate for use on our campus. To assess student development with respect to specified general education objectives, we administer the objective form of the ACT COMP. This exam yields a total score and six subscores, three of them in content areas (functioning in social institutions, using science and technology, and using the arts) and three in the process areas of communicating, solving problems, and clarifying values. Since 1983, we have been testing freshmen and seniors with this instrument. This year, for the first time, we have the longitudinal data that will permit us to measure growth by comparing ACT COMP scores for some of our seniors with the scores they obtained on the exam as freshmen. In the meantime, ACT has sent us four annual score profiles of our students that are remarkably similar. This consistency suggests that the ACT COMP is a reliable instrument. As a consequence, we have begun to use the score profiles to suggest directions for improving our general education curriculum.

To assess student achievement in the majors, we have asked faculty in 104 disciplines to agree on performance objectives for students finishing their programs and on priorities among content areas within the disciplines, and then either to locate or to develop comprehensive exams that meet the faculty-developed criteria. In approximately half of our program fields, faculty have access to standardized exams, and most have elected to use them. In 45 disciplines, however, faculty have designed their own exams in consultation with external content specialists (Banta and Schneider, in press). Whether tests are nationally standardized or developed locally, faculty are expected to interpret test scores and draw inferences for the improvement of curriculum, instruction, and such academic services as advising.

The Kellogg task force investigating ways of assessing the opinion of client groups decided, on the basis of some prior experience at UTK, that commercially available instruments would not yield information that campus decision makers would use extensively. Consequently, the university entered into a contract with two faculty specialists in survey research, who developed a series of related survey instruments for administration to enrolled undergraduates, enrolled graduate students, alumni, and dropouts.

The two survey developers studied a variety of existing instruments and then asked groups of student leaders, academic department heads and deans, and central administrators to review drafts of instruments. Each year since 1983, a new survey in the series has been developed, and we now have collected data from all four client groups. All the surveys contain sections that ask respondents about the extent of their use and the quality of various campuswide services, programs and services provided by academic departments, and aspects of classroom experience. Information from the surveys of undergraduate and graduate students is gathered for each department in the year before its comprehensive program review, so that each faculty can consider the indications of program quality that the surveys provide as it compiles its self-study.

Reactions to Assessment Findings

Administration of the ACT COMP to freshmen and seniors over four years has produced evidence that the scores of UTK students are lowest on functioning in social institutions and problem-solving. As a result, the social science component of the general education core curriculum has been strengthened. Moreover, an interdisciplinary group of faculty is exploring ways to implement a "problem solving across the curriculum" initiative.

Our surveys have revealed strengths and weaknesses both in academic departments and in the several student services that are centrally provided. As the surveys are administered repeatedly over time, we can assess the effectiveness of our efforts to improve in each of these areas. For example, a year ago, one-fourth of UTK dropouts indicated that they left the university because they could not get the advice they needed about courses and programs. A major initiative designed to improve advising was undertaken, and this year the number of enrolled students rating the "the willingness of adviser to help" as good or excellent was 7 percent higher.

The survey of enrolled undergraduates in departments scheduled for comprehensive program review showed that individual departments have made improvements in several areas, including printed information about programs, availability and quality of internships, opportunities for faculty-student interaction, student professional organizations, and faculty involvement in placement of graduates.

The development by faculty of comprehensive exams in the major fields is the assessment activity that has been most productive of change within departments. As a result of reaching a consensus about what students should know and be able to do when they finish their courses in the majors, faculty have attained greater consistency in the teaching of core courses and have improved the integration of lower- and upper-division course work. As UTK moves from a quarter-based toward a semester-based calendar in 1988, in some departments core competencies for students are being used to guide development of the semester curriculum. Some departments working with off-campus consultants on comprehensive exams have invited those consultants to conduct informal peer reviews. In almost every case, interaction with the off-campus consultants has been a stimulating experience for faculty working on the exams.

Once the locally developed comprehensive exams have been administered, faculty have been motivated by student performance to implement changes in curriculum and instruction. A stronger core curriculum has been established in several departments. Course requirements outside the department have been changed. For example, majors in one department had been encouraged to take a chemistry sequence for biology majors, but after administering its comprehensive exam, the faculty in that department decided that the chemistry sequence for chemistry majors would be more appropriate.

The objectives developed by faculty to guide test construction have been used to provide more structure for individual courses. Instructors are placing more emphasis on students' ability to apply their classroom learning. More written assignments, more opportunities to solve problems, more term projects, field trips, and internships are being used to increase students' abilities to solve problems and demonstrate other complex skills within the disciplines.

Finally, the comprehensive exams will provide data for comparing the relative effectiveness of the quarter-based and the semester-based calendars in promoting student achievement in the majors. After several administrations of the exams to graduates on the quarter calendar, scores can be compared with those of graduates completing majors on the semester calendar.

Four key assumptions underlie the UTK assessment program. First, we are evaluating the quality of our programs, not the achievement of individual students. Thus, we focus on mean scores and dispersion around the mean for the purpose of discovering program strengths and weaknesses, rather than looking at the scores of individual students for the purpose of making some decision about them. Students are asked to participate honestly in the evaluation activities designed to improve the university's programs. They are not penalized, however, for failing to attain some minimum level of performance.

Second, no single assessment technique can provide all the information needed to evaluate a program. Thus, several sources of data—test scores as well as survey responses—must be used.

Third, assessment information must be integrated and interpreted, disseminated widely, considered by decision makers, and then used to improve programs. This process can be expedited if a single individual or office with campuswide authority has responsibility for coordinating all assessment activities.

Finally, the campus assessment program must be trusted and supported at all levels, by students, faculty, and administrators. Administrators must assure students and faculty that assessment results will not be employed to eliminate weak programs but instead to focus improvement efforts. Students must participate openly and honestly in providing evaluation data, and faculty should review the results objectively and be guided by them as they make improvements.

A Faculty Perspective

The implementation of performance funding at UTK has had a benign effect on most faculty. Indeed, many of our colleagues are unaware of the extent of the program because it has caused so little disturbance of their day-to-day work. Nevertheless, there are particular circumstances in

Tennessee that have contributed to the faculty's acceptance of assessment programs here. First of all, there is a relatively high degree of trust between faculty and campus administrators, a trust accompanied by a tradition of top-down decision making. In addition, system-level administrators have a strong record of protecting our academic values from outside bureaucratic or legislative meddling. Relationships with the Tennessee Higher Education Commission (THEC) are generally cooperative, rather than combative.

Against this setting, Tennessee's performance funding program originated as a positive approach to educational assessment. It was designed to reward evaluation efforts and good results but not to punish failures. The program awards bonus money above that generated by formula funding. It is not an attempt to restrict institutions by taking money away. Every college or university in the state can qualify for 100 percent of its allocated sum without causing other campuses to receive diminished amounts. In addition, the assessment procedures on our campus do not result in finger-pointing; individual departments, course sequences, and faculty members are not singled out for public blame or praise as a result of test scores.

The ACT COMP measures how all undergraduate programs are contributing to our students' development of adult-level skills, rather than revealing how effective the freshman English sequence may be. Students' progress and graduation are not jeopardized by their scores on the ACT COMP or on exams in the major fields. Departments and colleges use assessment results to understand the impact of their programs and guide proposals for improvement. Strategic planners also find the information helpful in making institutional decisions. In short, outcomes assessment provides incentives for gathering accurate data and using the information to strengthen educational efforts.

The way in which assessment activities were implemented on our campus has also contributed to their success among faculty. The project began with a small-scale study, financed by grant money and approved by deans and campus administrators. Faculty were involved from the beginning, but the concept of outcomes evaluation itself was not put before the faculty senate for a vote. The enlargement of our assessment programs has been gradual and noncontroversial. Endorsement by the faculty senate has come through its approval of a requirement that students participate in assessment activities as a condition of graduation. Even when the construction of tests in the major fields has generated extra work for faculty, their reaction to assessment has generally been favorable because all faculty members have had the opportunity to see the results of evaluation surveys and tests and to make use of them in program planning. No one, of course, has complained about the extra money ($4.2 million last year) that UTK has received from the state as a direct result of our assessment projects.

Had any of these variables been different, the faculty's perception of and reaction to outcomes evaluation might also have been quite different. Thus, Tennessee's experience cannot necessarily be replicated elsewhere. If in the future the THEC changes the basis on which performance funding is dispensed—for example, by incorporating punitive measures into the procedure or by denying graduation to students who score low on standardized tests—our faculty may come to regard the whole program as an unjustifiable infringement of academic freedom. Our experience with performance funding, however, shows that faculty should work in concert with legislative and higher education authorities to ensure that assessment programs promote a better understanding of the aims of higher education while providing rewards to all campuses that seek to improve educational quality.

References

Association of American Colleges. "The Problem of Accountability." In *Integrity in the College Curriculum: A Report to the Academic Community*. Washington, D.C.: Association of American Colleges, 1985.

Banta, T. W. *Performance Funding in Higher Education: A Critical Analysis of Tennessee's Experience*. Boulder, Colo.: National Center for Higher Education Management Systems (NCHEMS), 1986.

Banta, T. W., and Schneider, J. "Using Faculty-Developed Comprehensive Exams for Majors in Program Assessment." *The Journal of Higher Education*, in press.

National Governors' Association. *Time for Results: The Governors' 1991 Report on Education*. Washington, D.C.: National Governors' Association Center for Policy Research and Analysis, 1986.

Southern Association of Colleges and Schools. *Criteria for Accreditation—Commission on Colleges*. Atlanta, Ga.: Southern Association of Colleges and Schools, 1984.

Study Group on the Conditions of Excellence in American Higher Education. *Involvement in Learning: Realizing the Potential of American Higher Education*. Washington, D.C.: National Institute of Education, 1984.

Trudy W. Banta is research professor in the Learning Research Center at the University of Tennessee, Knoxville, where she coordinates the university's instructional evaluation program.

Marian S. Moffett is professor of architecture and chair of the Educational Policies Committee of the Academic Senate at the University of Tennessee, Knoxville.

*A comprehensive assessment program informs, enlightens,
and becomes a basis for action. When put to work, it involves
every level and segment of the organization.*

Assessment and Involvement: Investments to Enhance Learning

Darrell W. Krueger, Margarita L. Heisserer

Assessment is the driving force within any realistic, systematic plan for institutional progress and development. Such an undertaking requires clear goals and objectives, a means of determining how closely the institution approximates the goals stated, and a strategy for closing the gaps that are identified. For this plan to be meaningful, the first two steps must be expressed in empirical, measurable terms. Otherwise, the whole process is reduced to mere rhetoric, and evaluations are totally subjective at best.

Useful, effective assessment measures in higher education can set in motion an institutional dynamic that permeates the entire system. For example, it prompts the university community to establish clearer, more comprehensible goals and objectives in fulfilling its mission and purposes. It provides a viable data base from which strategies for reducing gaps between the ideal and the current levels of performance may be readily deduced.

If the institution's goals and objectives are firmly committed to student growth and development, other benefits accrue. Identifying acceptable indications and levels of performance, as well as assessing the degree to which these standards are being met, stimulates the active involvement of students, faculty, and support personnel in one of the primary functions

D. F. Halpern (ed.). *Student Outcomes Assessment: What Institutions Stand to Gain.*
New Directions for Higher Education, no. 59. San Francisco: Jossey-Bass, Fall 1987.

of any university—learning. In fact, the entire learning environment—teaching, research, achievement, resources, and services—takes on a new, better-focused emphasis. Assessment becomes an interface between the goal and the reality of learning. It more clearly pinpoints the effectiveness or ineffectiveness of the university experience of students.

The expectations of the university community become clarified through assessment. When assessment programs are made known, a personal response from each member of the university community is sought, thus promoting total involvement. The assessment information used for making changes heightens involvement as each segment of the university is made aware of its condition. Assessment maps out the trends, values, and impacts of the university experience so that the university knows better what it is, what it is doing, and what it can, will or should become.

When building an assessment program, a university needs to build a program uniquely adapted to its own mission and goals. Both the theory and the practice of assessment must be clearly defined before a program of assessment can be satisfactorily implemented. The purposes must be meaningful, the processes relevant, and the performance outcomes valid.

Essential to a successful outcomes assessment program is the use of multiple measures. A single test or questionnaire may help to raise important questions about the university, program, or student, but the questions will largely be rationalized away unless other, reinforcing information can be collected. As soon as other information about the significant question is collected, plausible answers may begin to appear. In general, the more measures collected—by means of different instruments that point to the same conclusion—the more certain the observer can feel about the conclusion that is reached. This process of using multiple measures to focus on problem areas is called *triangulation*.

In the early 1970s, Northeast Missouri State University (NMSU) at Kirksville chose a value-added approach to assessment. Primarily a strong undergraduate state-supported institution, NMSU was guided by three fundamental goals in the development of its assessment program: to know everything possible about each student, to demonstrate that the university experience makes a positive difference in the student's life, and to evaluate the integrity of the degree and demonstrate that graduates are nationally competitive in their fields. The target of assessment was student learning. The unfolding of that assessment plan, begun in 1973, has changed NMSU.

The Value-Added Approach to Assessment

In November 1984, the North Central Evaluation Visiting Team cited the value-added concept and its use in assessment in its evaluation report. The team viewed the value-added approach as a tool or catalyst for the improvement of student learning.

In brief, the value-added approach is the institution's commitment to be accountable to students, and its other constituencies, by providing an education which demonstrably improves their knowledge and abilities through programs which are, or will be perceived as, nationally competitive. . . . This approach benefits the educational process in several ways, two of which are described here. First, it provides a data base on academic performance of students and therefore becomes a quality assurance system for the educational process. The data base has become a means for faculty to crystallize what they are looking for in students and to track them through the institution. In effect, it enables faculty to raise questions about the curriculum and to institute appropriate refinements and revisions. . . .

A second benefit of this approach is that the focus on ensuring improvement in student learning provides an integrating process for the university in areas related to the teaching-learning process. Questions related to improving student performance direct the goals and activities of other campus offices, e.g. recruitment, admissions, advising. Because the goals of the value-added approach are public, it is possible, and has become practice, for all units of the university to employ this integrating idea in evaluating unit goals and objectives [Curtis and others, 1985, pp. 8–9].

The strengths of the program are summarized in a joint consulting report by Banta and Ewell (1985) as part of the NCHEMS/Kellogg Dissemination Project:

It is *comprehensive,* in that it covers major aspects of the university experience; it is *straightforward,* in that it is easy for all parties to understand its mechanisms and intent; and it is *simple,* making use for the most part of standardized "off the shelf" measurement instruments as the basis for assessment. With the assessment program as a centerpiece, the university has been able to considerably enhance its academic quality, and consequently, its standing among its peers. . . .

[There is] evident enthusiasm and interest among faculty in linking assessment with instruction. . . . First, the language of assessment is now a natural language for institutional discourse at every level; faculty and administrators alike seem both comfortable and facile with this language, and recognize it as a unifying theme in addressing questions of instructional improvement. Secondly, the assessment program has helped establish a notable level of self-confidence and identification with the institution.

Banta and Ewell further noted that positive change has occurred at NMSU as a result of the assessment program.

> In evaluating its broad impact at NMSU, however, it is important to recall exactly what the value-added assessment program was intended to accomplish. . . . Developments suggest that much of the original intent of the assessment program at NMSU may already have been accomplished. . . . NMSU has an opportunity to build on success. Basic acceptance of the assessment program throughout the university and accumulation of many years of assessment information in computer-accessible files allow NMSU to investigate the causes of different patterns of student performance in much more sophisticated ways. Current day reporting and analysis allows easy identification of success and failure in the curriculum. Accumulated data bases and the use of multivariate analytical techniques will allow investigation of the reasons behind these results [pp. 8–9].

In a further study of the assessment program of NMSU, Kurfiss and Silvernail (1986) submitted the following summary:

> The NMSU program is commendable for many reasons. . . .
> 1. Clear vision and commitment to purpose on the part of administrators, faculty, and staff. . . .
> 2. The extensive use of assessment information as a cornerstone in fulfilling the institutional mission
> 3. An impressive record of using assessment information for assessing and improving the quality of the NMSU program
> 4. Strong, supportive leadership on the part of the president and upper-level administrative staff
> 5. A high level of faculty involvement in the process of program analysis and development
> 6. Easy and widespread access to all assessment information for faculty, administrators, and staff
> 7. A conscious and continuous effort to encourage all college personnel to engage in analysis and use of assessment information
> 8. The creation of an environment and practices which encourage and reward involvement rather than using information in a punitive fashion

9. The recogition that any assessment tool has limitations and should be used wisely
10. The use of a triangulation model in collecting several types of assessment information in order to more accurately identify the potential nature and scope of problem areas
11. The collection, analysis, and use of information on attitudes and satisfaction levels to assist in assessing the overall quality of the program
12. The commitment to using a value-added model for assessing and improving the quality of the NMSU program
13. The quality and professionalism of all personnel. Regardless of title or responsibilities, [all] staff are viewed . . . as instructional leaders
14. The recognition on the part of NMSU that improving program quality is a continuing process, rather than an objective to be accomplished. Program improvement is seen as a developmental process requiring time and resources, sensitivity to staff development needs, reflective thought, cooperation, and leaders committed to leading by example and by support [pp. 6-7].

Three parts of NMSU's student assessment program have been rather widely publicized across the nation. One is the value-added component, which seeks to demonstrate student growth in general knowledge between the beginning of the freshman year and the end of the sophomore year through successive administrative of the ACT and the ACT COMP. Another is the comparative achievement component, which seeks to demonstrate student achievement in the major fields by means of a senior test. The senior test is a nationally recognized and administered test, such as a GRE field examination or a professional certification test. The senior test, administered to all students at the end of the senior year, is required for graduation. The third part is the attitudinal component, which seeks to determine students' perceptions of their own growth and their evaluations of the university and its services by means of a variety of questionnaire surveys administered at different points in the undergraduate career. These range from initial orientation surveys to graduation, alumni, and employer surveys.

Less well known is NMSU's recent use of the ETS placement examination; the ACT COMP writing examination; the ACT COMP speaking examination; other national exams, such as the ACS national chemistry exam; numerous local outcome measures within programs, such as the physical education program, to ensure minimum skills in a variety of areas; and instruments such as the Myer-Briggs Personality Inventory. These student assessment items, when used with demographic and other traditionally collected student assessment data, such as grades and course-taking history, are excellent in helping every aspect of the university change, improve, and evaluate effectiveness.

Assessment and Involvement

The Student Level. Student assessment data can be effectively used at every level of the university. Of course, the focal point of the data is the student. The data can increase student involvement in learning outcomes, institutional issues, and discipline activities, as well as increasing the level of student satisfaction with the university. Astin (1984) has stated:

> Student involvement refers to the quantity and quality of the physical and psychological energy that students invest in the college experience. Such involvement takes many forms, such as absorption in academic work, participation in extracurricular activities, and interaction with faculty and other institutional personnel. According to the theory, the greater the student's involvement in the college, the greater will be the amount of student learning and personal development. From the standpoint of the educator, the most important hypothesis in the theory is that the effectiveness of any educational policy or practice is directly related to the capacity of the policy or practice to increase student involvement [p. 307].

Increased involvement in learning outcomes is evidence by test score gains, amount of time spent studying, frequency of discussion with other students, use of the library, and frequency of revising writing.

Since 1975, freshman and sophomore testing data have been collected on students in matched sequence, originally using the Sequential Test of Educational Progress (STEP) and, since 1979, the ACT and the ACT COMP. The longitudinal year-to-year pattern of the composite and subtest scores indicates an improved impact over time. Since 1973, graduating seniors have taken senior examinations appropriate for their major areas of study. As individual disciplines gather longitudinal data, gains are noted. In accounting, for example, the American Institute of Certified Public Accountants Level II test is administered to graduating seniors. Since 1980, when 48 percent scored above the 50th percentile, there have been steady gains, with 72 percent scoring above the 50th percentile in 1986.

Students are spending more independent time on learning. In 1982, a university sampling of 436 students reflected that only 9 percent studied more than twenty hours per week, with 24 percent studying sixteen hours or more. In 1986, with 1,490 students in the sample, 23.5 percent studied more than twenty hours per week, with 48 percent studying sixteen hours or more.

Although only three years of data are available on the frequency of discussion with other students on serious topics and the frequency of revising to improve style and techniques of writing, the longitudinal pattern indicates improved impact. The number of times students involved themselves in intellectual activities varied, with the cited activity of "used library resources to gather research materials and information" showing a consistent universitywide longitudinal upward trend for 1984, 1985, and 1986 of 2.55, 2.78, and 2.90, respectively, on a 4.00 scale, with 4.00 indicating once a week or more.

Still another indication of students' increased involvement is their growing interest in institutionwide educational issues. The student senate at NMSU plays an active role in issues related to education. Over the years, it has passed resolutions that have been referred to the faculty senate for action. In the spring of 1982, a resolution was passed to support the faculty and administration in any effort to raise academic standards. A resolution was passed later, asking the faculty to study the possibility of establishing a "dead week" before final exams. Another resolution asked that longer library hours be established. Still another established a committee to hold hearings on value-added considerations and make recommendations on improving student learning. More recently, a standing committee of the student senate on academic affairs has been established to work closely with faculty and administrators in strengthening the academic program of the university. During the past semester, the student senate made arrangements for late-night study facilities during finals week and sponsored forums about the new mission of the university.

Students are members of all faculty constitutional committees and are appointed by the student senate president. The number of students seeking election and appointment has increased, and participation in student senate elections has increased. A regular nonvoting member of the board of governors is a student selected by the students, with final appointment by the governor of Missouri. The number of students attending the open meetings of the board has increased.

Students are involved not only in universitywide concerns but also in academic discipline activities. Members of the student senate have become interested in academic division meetings and discussions and are now able to provide feedback to and from the student body. Curriculum meetings of the academic areas are frequently attended by students, and a student representative from the major is a regular member of each discipline curriculum committee. Faculty and student interaction and interchange are enhanced by this interest.

Students volunteer as peer counselors in their disciplines, providing an important informational service to their fellow students. Involvement in student orientation activities has been heightened as a result of the assessment process. Students feel good about informing incoming students that they should make every effort to take advantage of university experiences and that the assessment program of the university will let them know how they are doing. Student volunteers are pleased to be asked and readily assist in the leadership conferences held in the fall for freshmen in each academic division. Students feel honored to be called upon to represent their divisions or the university in forums on the assessment program that are presented at conferences, meetings and workshops, both on and off campus. Another spinoff of the assessment program is students' heightened interest in and expectations of academic advisement. Revisions in divisional advisement programs were hastened because of student requests for improvement. Students seem to be more earnest as they evaluate classroom experiences. They take very seriously their role in the hiring of new faculty, which is to provide their impressions to the division head regarding applicants being considered for employment. Students share their impressions after attending classes taught by prospective faculty members.

Student satisfaction, as measured by survey instruments, has increased, particularly in programs that have heavy student involvement. In psychology, for example, there has been an improvement in students' attitudes toward courses in the major and toward the quality of instruction, as measured on an institutional survey. The mean score went from 2.82 in 1980 to 3.39 in 1986 on a 4.00 scale for the question "How satisfied were you with the courses in your major?" For satisfaction with the quality of instruction in the major, the mean score went from 2.97 to 3.32 on a 4.00 scale. At the same time, the proportion scoring above the 50th percentile on the senior exam (GRE in psychology) went from 18 percent in 1981 to 67 percent in 1986.

In nursing, the senior test scores stayed consistently high, while the attitudes of students toward the program improved and then leveled off much higher than commonly found universitywide. The senior test scores never dropped below 93 percent passage on the state boards, and for three of the last five years, 100 percent of the students passed the boards. At the same time, student attitudes toward courses in the major improved dramatically. In 1980, our graduating student questionnaire indicated a mean score of 2.40; in 1986, the mean score was 3.50, while the university average was 3.30. Similarly, the students' attitudes toward the quality of instruction went from 2.30 to 3.40; the university average in 1986 was 3.20. The nursing faculty went to great lengths to increase interaction with students outside of the formal classroom setting. The division head met individually with all seniors, and more input was sought from all students. The increased interaction of faculty and students made a positive difference in stimulating student satisfaction.

The Discipline Level. Assessment promotes reflection on teaching methods. It also raises questions about the curriculum. As Ewell (1983) has stated in a consulting report, "Because of the presence of the program and the explicit data that it provides, the discussions of improving the effectiveness of individual academic programs are allowed to be refreshingly concrete. Casting instructional objectives in terms of explicit outcomes criteria, for example, is a good way of fostering clear and critical thinking about curriculum and about teaching on the part of faculty and division heads. . . . Continued discussion *about* assessment is at least as important as assessment itself in raising the kinds of issues necessary for improving instructional quality" (pp. 2, 8).

When put to work, outcomes assessment requires faculty to look at the connection between objectives and outcomes. Involvement in assessment helps faculty to specify the outcomes they expect from their students in individual courses and in the programs of their disciplines. The stimulus of outcomes data prompted the chemistry faculty at NMSU to increase learning in chemistry by adopting some of the thinking of Ausebel (1978), as interpreted by Novak and Gowin (1984). The essential theme of this theory is that students should be taught to construct their own knowledge schemes within the disciplines by means of concept mapping. The most progress in this plan has been made in organic chemistry, where students have shown improvements in classroom exam scores of up to 70 percent in areas where they have been taught and encouraged to do concept mapping.

In English, faculty have struggled with students' competency in writing and speaking. From its inception, the value-added model of assessment has given impetus to the improvement of writing in every discipline on campus. Discussions on outcomes data provided a setting for cooperation among faculties of the various divisions and created an environment for a number of things to happen institutionally. Discipline faculty discussed the problem with the composition faculty, who became the controlling resource. Professors across the campus began to require more writing in their courses. Consistent and persistent efforts toward correct writing became the norm across campus, and writing was not the sole responsibility of the instructor of Composition I. Workshops were offered by the composition faculty to faculty of other divisions. Writing became a vehicle to enhance the higher-order thinking processes and was seen by students and faculty members as a skill in which continuous growth occurred throughout the total university experience, giving added integrity to undergraduate degrees. Competency in writing was made a graduation requirement by the various university councils.

In psychology, response to feedback regarding how much students were actually learning prompted the psychology faculty to define the subject matter of the discipline, strengthen the curriculum, implement higher standards, move to more valid in-class assessment, provide for a comprehensive exit review of the basic content of the discipline, and provide generous encouragement to individual students who achieve. The psychology faculty have become actively involved in improving all aspects of their courses.

In most of the majors, the results of the senior tests, along with the survey data and the experience of the faculty, have caused faculty to reevaluate all courses and sequencing of courses in the majors so that the essential elements of the discipline are being taught, and to ensure that the curriculum is sufficiently rigorous for graduates to be nationally competitive. In attempting to upgrade the curriculum in biology, to help students become more competitive nationally, the faculty first initiated a new course in cell biology for all majors at the sophomore level. Next, they introduced two new required sequence courses in biology for freshmen. These two course identify the principal unifying ideas of the science and illustrate some of the evidence supporting these ideas. They also provide students with opportunities to experience the intellectual processes central to scientific thought.

If faculty have evaluated the curriculum, reviewed their teaching methods, and increased involvement of students in the learning process, then advisement also becomes an agenda item, especially when surveys reveal a trend of increased dissatisfaction with advisement. Our students were expecting more from the advisement system. As pressure increased to study more, and as the curriculum was being changed to eliminate "soft" tracks and courses, students felt the strain. They wanted and expected more time with the adviser, time in which the adviser would help them deal with these pressures and help them integrate available resources with individual goals. To help address these concerns, central advisement workshops were held for lead advisers from each discipline. Once the workshops were completed, the lead advisers were expected to return to their own disciplines and conduct similar workshops. Peer advisement programs were developed, and an extended fall orientation program for freshmen was begun.

Through the assessment program at NMSU, considerable data are available on the nature of the students in each discipline. Data are available not only on the types of students being taught—ability levels, geographical origins, and high school curricular and extracurricular achievements—but also on the attitudes of students toward a wide variety of issues. There are also data on the performance of students on nationally normed and locally developed tests. These data help the faculty determine what direction they wish their programs to take and, once they have initiated change, to see whether the changes are having the desired results. In sum, faculty have become even more involved in their disciplines. Rather than giving actual direction, the data aid in the decision-making process and help give feedback on results of decisions that are implemented.

The University Level. At the university level, NMSU's value-added assessment program has provided the data, attitudes, and values that are essential for long-range planning. The program has helped direct the university and provided feedback on the direction the university has taken. The outcomes assessment data have facilitated program review and institutional accreditations.

The institutional attitudes and values that encourage long-range planning are often hard to develop, especially when no noticeable results are readily seen. Many institutions write long-range plans and then shelve them; little ever comes of such plans besides the very positive relationships developed during the planning effort. At NMSU, the planning environment has developed around the use of outcomes data. As a consequence, planning becomes almost continuous: As data are updated, immediate feedback is given about whether the goals are being achieved. In many instances, goals can be updated on a regular basis. Anticipation even develops about whether a given goal will begin to be realized, as the data seem to show. Moreover, self-interest, self-involvement, and institutional reinforcement cause movement toward future ideals through current action and belief that goals are within reach.

Direction for change is also provided by outcomes data. Data are longitudinal, and so policymakers at the university have information that allows them to determine how well they are doing in regard to improving the student body, the learning environment, and the involvement of students and faculty in the learning processes. This information aids in determining the university's direction and in showing what changes would aid in increasing desired outcomes.

Assessment also helps involve the professional staff in the mission, objectives, and goals of the university. Students have been asked on questionnaires, "How satisfied were you with the experiences, services, and facilities at NMSU?" The admissions office, registrar's office, financial aid office, career/placement office, student activities office, and so on, became more interested in meeting the needs of students and identifying ways to support the university effort. On the early student questionnaires, for example, the library received the highest evaluation on campus. Starting in 1976, however, there was a decrease in the mean evaluation score of the library each year. The staff and the facility were the same all those years, but library use increased, and holdings were expanded, which caused loss of study space. It also caused shelving problems. Thus, students reflected less and less satisfaction with library services. These data were added to the proposal for the current renovation and expansion of the university library.

56

Conclusion

Assessment and involvement promote each other. A comprehensive assessment program informs, enlightens, and becomes a basis for action. When put to work, it involves every level and segment of the organization.

At NSMU, assessment has increased the involvement of students, faculty, staff, and administrators in improving learning outcomes and student attitudes toward the university and its functions. Through assessment, the university has been able to document its positive influence on students and have a demonstrable impact on their total development.

References

Astin, A. W. "Student Involvement: A Developmental Theory for Higher Education." *Journal of College Student Personnel*, 1984, 25 (4), 307.

Ausebel, D. *Education Psychology: A Cognitive View*. (2d ed.) New York: Holt, Rinehart & Winston, 1978.

Banta, T., and Ewell, P. T. Unpublished campus consulting report, Northeast Missouri State University, 1985.

Curtis, D. V., Carroll, M. A., Doherty, A., Runnalls, N. G., and Harris, J. Unpublished report of a visit to Northeast Missouri State University for the Commission on Institutions of Higher Education of the North Central Association of Colleges and Schools, 1985.

Ewell, P. T. Unpublished consulting report, Northeast Missouri State University, 1983.

Kurfiss, J., and Silvernail, D. L. Unpublished report of the Assessment Program Evaluation of Northeast Missouri State University, 1986.

Novak, J. D., and Gowin, D. B. *Learning How to Learn*. New York: Cambridge University Press, 1984.

Darrell W. Krueger is dean of instruction at Northeast Missouri State University. He directs and is responsible for the implementation of the value-added assessment program of the university.

Margarita L. Heisserer, administrative assistant to the dean of instruction, works with documentation and dissemination of the assessment program.

*To assess outcomes, we must overcome enormous problems of
procedure and analysis, but we cannot refuse to look at what
the instruments enable us to see.*

Assessing General Education: Trenton State College

Wade Curry, Elizabeth Hager

For the past twelve years, New Jersey has been testing all college freshmen for basic skills and providing enriched funding for remedial courses.
The state Board of Higher Education has now mandated the testing of
outcomes and established a committee to carry it out. That committee
has rejected the so-called Florida Plan, in which the test is the only
gateway into the junior year. Such a test, the committee believes, would
necessarily force colleges to concentrate on a narrow set of skills and on
the very lowest standards. Instead, the committee recommends that New
Jersey focus on improving academic programs through four kinds of
assessment.

1. The final exams for remedial courses will be similar to the
   original basic skills test.
2. A statewide test will focus on thinking skills.
3. Each college will assess the knowledge areas of its general
   education program.
4. Each college will assess the effectiveness of its major programs.

This chapter reports on research conducted by Henry Wang. The authors
thank Paul Cruser, who contributed significantly to their analysis and report.

D. F. Halpern (ed.). *Student Outcomes Assessment: What Institutions Stand to Gain.*
New Directions for Higher Education, no. 59. San Francisco: Jossey-Bass, Fall 1987.

Faculty Survey

At Trenton State College, a committee chaired by Elizabeth Hager carried out a pilot assessment of our general education program. The committee was charged with determining whether and to what extent students achieved the college's eight general education goals. After revising the goals, the committee surveyed all departments that offered general education courses, asking to what extent their courses met each goal and how departments did or could evaluate student achievement of these goals. Each member of the committee met with one or two departments to explain the kind of information that was desired and how it would be used. Faculty were invited to appear before the committee to clarify their responses.

There was considerable resistance. Faculty assumed that the information would be used in personnel decisions or in determining which courses would remain in the general education distribution. Committee members tried to reassure faculty that the committee's purpose was only to get information about the current state of the curriculum.

The results were interesting, after the committee clarified that there was no advantage in reporting that a course met all eight goals and that "moderate" emphasis did not mean a few words in a lecture. Several courses did not stress the goals that seemed their natural responsibilities. For example, most humanities courses did not stress values clarification, and some stressed neither Western nor Eastern culture. In courses for which more than one faculty member responded, there were sometimes very different profiles. It seemed to the committee that faculty should have the greatest freedom to choose materials, examples, theories, and teaching methods, but that they should still agree on the goals of a course.

The results of the survey are summarized in Table 1. The faculty reported that our general education program emphasizes communication and research and problem solving. The least emphasis, they reported, was on the arts and non-Western civilization.

Testing of Students

A second thrust of the committee was to assess student learning. Two of the faculty on the committee argued vigorously against any testing program. They made the following points.

1. About half of our seniors are transfer students who took general education at other colleges.
2. Our general education is a loose distribution of over one hundred courses from which students or their departments select fifteen. How can one test a distribution?

Table 1. Survey Results

Goal	Average[a]
Communication and research	2.10
Problem solving	2.10
Values clarification	1.44
Social sciences	1.33
Mathematics, science, and technology	1.34
Arts	0.86
Western civilization	1.26
Non-Western civilization	0.83

[a] Very Strong = 3, Moderate = 1, Not at all = 0

3. Gains made over four years may result from variables other than classroom instruction. The less motivated freshmen will drop out, while the more motivated learners who remain will read widely and use their leisure for activities that develop their intellectual abilities.
4. The tests may simply measure intelligence. If so, they are a better measure of what the students bring to the college than what the college's program offers them.

These are all good arguments. The committee agreed with them but said, "Let's do it anyway." In the end, the majority of the committee agreed that a grant should be sought to run a pilot test. Now that the pilot has been run, we must not only agree with those four arguments but add five more.

1. If the test does not affect grade point average or graduation, some students will not try hard. A few of their essays were gibberish, although most students did seem to try hard.
2. The four-hour test came at the end of a twelve-hour day for most students. By ten o'clock, they were tired and irritable.
3. It is difficult to get people to give up four hours when there is no personal gain. We required the test, but a typical response was, "What will happen to me if I don't take it?" Only 70 percent of the students in our sample took the test, biasing the sample. Many of the better seniors did not take the test.
4. We could find no test that evaluates all the skills and understandings that we consider important. (It is probably impossible to construct such a test. One solution is that of Alverno College, which conducts many assessments, using a variety of methods.)

5. We were unprepared for the small differences in raw scores between freshmen and seniors. On the ACT COMP, the average difference is eight points on the total and two on each subtest category. At midrange in a subtest category, a two-point difference in raw score moves the student about 15 percentiles.

These nine procedural problems are extremely difficult to solve. We suggest that enthusiasm be tempered by intelligence and skepticism, that results be interpreted with caution, and that several forms of assessment be used.

In any assessment program, the first step is to gain agreement on goals. The next step is to compare goals with the tests available. As Table 2 indicates, there are not many choices.

Table 2. Trenton State College Goals Compared with Available Tests

	GRE	Miller Analogy	NTE	CLEP	Under-graduate Assessment Program	ACT COMP	TGE
Communication and research	X	O	X	X	O	X	X
Problem solving	X	X	O	O	X	X	X
Values clarification	O	O	O	O	O	X	O
Social sciences	O	½X	X	X	X	X	O
Math, science, technology	½X	½X	X	X	½X	½X	X
Arts	O	½X	X	X	X	½X	O
Western civilization	O	O	X	X	X	O	O
Non-Western civilization	O	O	O	O	O	O	O
Subscores	X	O	O	X	X	X	X
Validated	X	X	X	X	X	X	O
National norms	X	X	X	X	X	X	O
Essay	O	O	X	X	O	O	X
Time	210	50	240	495	120	100	160

We were able to find only two tests designed to assess general education: The ACT COMP and the Test of General Education (TGE) from Educational Testing Service. What is worse, the TGE has not been normed and is still considered experimental. Several tests were eliminated from consideration because they did not provide subtest scores, and we felt that a single test score would not tell us much. The area examination from the College-Level Examination Program (CLEP) has some appeal because it covers knowledge areas broadly, but it is far too long. The GRE has a number of supporters, but it seems to us a poor choice; it is intended to discriminate at the upper end of the range. For example, on the GRE chemistry examination, a perfect score results from getting two-thirds of the answers. If we had to choose, we would prefer that the test discriminate best at the lower end of the scale, so that we could be sure that our students graduated with certain intellectual skills. The Miller Analogy is a good test of intelligence and is therefore useful as an admissions test, but not as an assessment test. The general examination of the National Teachers Examination (NTE) equates well with our goals and is a fairly good test (except of critical thinking); however, at the time we were considering it, Educational Testing Service would not provide subscores. The Undergraduate Assessment Program, like the GRE, seems to be a selection test and not an outcomes measurement device.

We were left with the ACT COMP and the TGE. The ACT COMP is geared to testing how a person will function as an adult, and our aim as colleges is to help students function effectively as adults. Nevertheless, if one were to ask sociology professors if they were teaching students how to function effectively in social institutions, the professors would say, "No, we are teaching sociology." For that reason, the ACT COMP is not a very good measure of what is actually being taught. A second weakness is that with each question, the testers are measuring three different goals. The questions cannot be too specific or too hard (for example, there cannot be any questions on classical music or on calculus) because information would be lost in three different areas.

The TGE concentrates on four intellectual skills and does not measure content. It has not been validated or normed, and we do not know what ETS plans to do with it.

We decided that we wanted to compare our native seniors with our transfer seniors, our native seniors with national norms, our native seniors with our freshmen, and our freshmen with their scores as seniors (in three years). We also wanted to compare the TGE and the ACT COMP. Because our faculty were most concerned about weaknesses in writing, we gave the essay examination from the TGE to students taking the ACT COMP, as well as to those taking the objective TGE.

On the ACT COMP, the difference between our samples of seniors and freshmen was eight raw score points—about average, but not enough

Table 3. ACT COMP Mean Percentiles
for TSC Freshmen and Seniors on National Norms

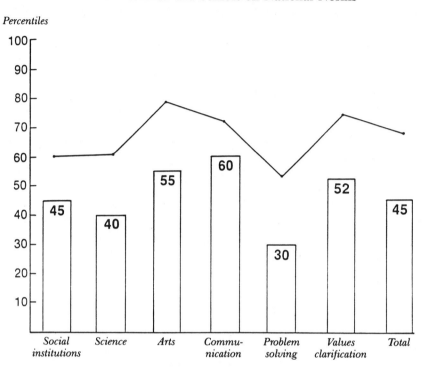

to give us much confidence in the results. In percentiles, the way ACT and individual colleges always present it, the gain seems huge. In actuality, it is not.

Table 3 compares our students with national norms for freshmen. What we see is not what the faculty expected; they remain unconvinced. They ask, "If this writing is at the 60th percentile, what must it be like to teach in the rest of the country?" Communication, however, appears to be an area of strength for our students. Faculty had reported that they put the least emphasis on values clarification and the arts, yet those too are areas of strength for our students. The most obvious "valley" on the chart is problem solving, which our faculty say they strongly emphasize. The line graph of senior scores shows the same configuration as that of the freshmen. Thus, students leave with almost the same competencies they had when they entered; they do not remedy their weaknesses. Why should we expect them to? The elective curriculum permits them to select courses in which they already have strength. College is designed to strengthen strengths and to let students avoid courses in which weaknesses will be revealed. Is that what we intended?

There are no national norms for the TGE. We compared our students to those at a state university. Their weakest thinking skill was integration, but they did better than the university students on the other three skills. This weakness makes sense. Our general education program is a series of discrete introductions to disciplines. Few courses have "hooks" out to other disciplines, nor do they require students to integrate what they have learned, but they should.

Our biggest surprise was that the difference between our men and our women was greater than the difference between our freshmen and our seniors. As Table 4 shows, females far outscored males in communication, and males far outscored females in mathematics. The students enter and leave with the same skills. Apparently, the average woman is not going to take courses that require quantitative work, and the average man is not going to take courses that require writing. Students perceive not a need to remediate weaknesses, but a need to avoid revealing weaknesses.

Table 4. TGE: Male/Female Senior Comparison of Skills

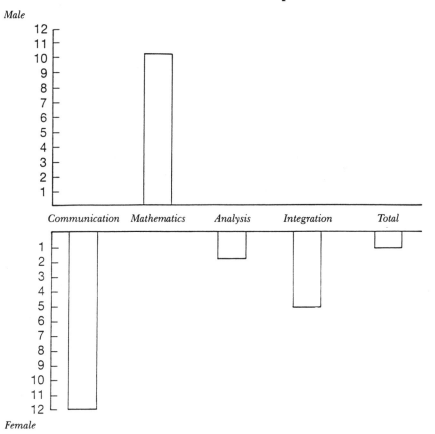

On the eight essays, our seniors usually scored far higher than our freshmen. Our major concern, however, was that about 20 percent to 30 percent of the seniors scored low on each question. While this group did not always comprise the same students, there was enough consistency to make us feel that a significant number of seniors (perhaps 10 percent to 15 percent) graduate without good communication skills and without cultural awareness. We think that we should be more concerned about those students than about whether our average student is above or below national norms.

There was no significant difference between our native and our transfer seniors. That surprised us, since we are very selective, and we have open-door community colleges in our state.

Conclusions

Are the ACT COMP and the TGE good tests? The total score on the ACT COMP revealed a good (but not outstanding) correlation with the grade point average (.36) and the SAT score (.43). The correlations of the six subscores with the total score were very high, as one would expect, since each question measures three skills. The correlations of the TGE with the grade point average (.47) and with the SAT (.61) are considerably higher than those of the ACT COMP, and the correlations of each test with the total score are also high. Of the two tests, we prefer the TGE because it seems to do a better job of isolating intellectual skills and because the raw scores ranges are greater. Some of the distinctions made by the ACT COMP seem somewhat dubious. For example, the higher-order communication skills branch over into critical thinking and artistic expression. How could our students score so high on communication and so low on problem solving when the two areas of skill are so closely related?

Is assessment worth doing, when one considers all the problems involved in getting a good test and a good sample of students? Our experience would seem to provide a resounding *yes*. After all, we found that our students did not demonstrate the skills that the faculty claimed to be stressing, nor did students show the weaknesses that faculty expected. The assessment also provided clear evidence that our courses will have to be delivered so that students must develop the intellectual skills required to pass them.

The assessment process is not a way of evaluating the individual student or the individual professor; it is a way of evaluating our program. To us, the process is a six-step feedback loop: develop or revise goals, attach the goals to each general education course, select or create a means of assessment, administer it and analyze the results, evaluate the instrument, evaluate and revise the curriculum. Then revise the goals, and continue.

Wade Curry is dean of arts and sciences at Trenton State College.

Elizabeth Hager is associate professor of biology at Trenton State College.

*State-imposed educational reforms, including mandatory
entry and exit testing, have had a major impact on Florida
institutions of higher education.*

Mandated Testing in Florida: A Faculty Perspective

Ana Alejandre Ciereszko

Presenting the faculty viewpoint of entry/exit testing is a challenging task because each faculty member, even within a single institution, has been affected in a different way. Some faculty who teach senior and graduate-level courses at large universities have not been affected by these changes, but faculty who teach freshmen and sophomores, whether at four-year schools or at community colleges, have had incredible demands placed on them. Even in community colleges, some faculty members' workload has increased tremendously, while others have not been affected much.

Florida initiated educational reforms in the early 1980s. After changes were made in curriculum and graduation requirements for secondary schools, the process was extended to higher education. The College-Level Academic Skills Test (CLAST) was developed as a "rising junior" exam, as directed by the Florida state legislature in 1982. Satisfactory scores have been required of students since 1983. In 1985, the Department of Education mandated testing of all first-time-in-college students and established scores below which students are required to enroll in college preparatory courses.

At Miami–Dade Community College, the impact of entry/exit testing cannot be separated from other major changes. In 1975, a major study on general education was initiated (Lukenbill and McCabe, 1978). A

D. F. Halpern (ed.). *Student Outcomes Assessment: What Institutions Stand to Gain.*
New Directions for Higher Education, no. 59. San Francisco: Jossey-Bass, Fall 1987.

general education program was developed over three years, involving most of the administration and faculty at the institution. There are three basic components to the program: entry assessment and placement, computer-based support systems, and monitoring of student flow.

Entry Assessment

Entry assessment has always occurred at Miami–Dade Community College. The difference effected by the general education program is that placement in the appropriate level became mandatory. Instead of just advising students who needed college preparatory work, but allowing them to actually choose the level they preferred (the "right to fail" approach), we now require students to enroll for the courses they need. Recognizing that tests do not always accurately predict a student's level, since the student may not have been physically or psychologically prepared on the day of the basic skills assessment, a second screening occurs in college preparatory courses on the first day of class. In English classes, the student produces a writing sample, while in reading and mathematics courses, a second placement exam is given. The faculty may then advise a student, if necessary, to change to a more appropriate course. This procedure provides some flexibility in the placement process.

Miami–Dade Community College (1985) surveyed faculty to determine their agreement or disagreement with basic skills testing and placement. Faculty overwhelmingly agreed that placement testing should occur, not to exclude underprepared students but to place those students at appropriate levels. Previously, students with wide differences in ability had been enrolled in identical courses. Faculty members often had to make a very difficult decision: whether to teach courses at the levels originally intended or at levels that the majority of the students could handle. Differences in ability still occur, but they are usually less pronounced (see Table 1).

General Education Program

The general education curriculum was implemented in 1983. There is a three-tiered approach: five core courses, a set of distribution courses from which to choose, and electives (see Table 2). Enrollment in the core courses is very high, since most beginning students enroll in one or more of them during the first semester of college. This prescribed ordering of courses, coupled with mandatory placement in college preparatory courses, has caused a major shift from higher-level courses—the electives that faculty most enjoy teaching—to basic skills courses and the general education core. The number of sections and the variety of electives have both decreased dramatically in the past five years. A review committee has just been established to study possible adjustments to the general education curriculum.

Table 1. Number and Proportion of "Agree" Responses from Faculty

Area Examined	Collegewide n	%
Students should pass a basic skills test before enrolling at the college	182	47
Placement testing should not be used at the college	15	4
Placement scores should be uniform throughout Florida	314	84
Developmental courses should be required	373	94
Classroom performance is unrelated to placement test scores	72	18
Good high school grades should exempt students from placement testing	75	19
A.A. degree or higher should exempt students from placement testing	298	75
Placement policies are applied consistently	90	44
Placement policies should be applied consistently	381	96
Placement test scores should be used for advisement only	72	18
The college should continue offering developmental classes	396	94

Table 2. General Education Program

Core Courses
English Composition I
Humanities
The Individual in Transition
The Social Environment
Energy in the Natural Environment

Distribution Courses
English Composition II
Advanced Composition
Social Science (a specific course from history, psychology, sociology, anthropology, government, or economics)
Natural Science (a specific course from biology, chemistry, physics, or earth science)
Humanities (a specific course from art, drama, literature, or philosophy)
Intermediate Algebra or higher mathematics
General College Mathematics

Elective Courses

Another part of the survey (Miami–Dade Community College, 1985) indicates that most faculty, particularly those who teach English composition and mathematics, support mandatory placement of students in college preparatory courses prior to enrollment in the core courses (see Table 3).

College-Level Academic Skills Test

The College-Level Academic Skills Test (CLAST) is an evaluation instrument with four components: an essay, and objective examinations in reading, writing, and computation. It determines whether a student can obtain an associate of arts degree after two years of college work and whether a student at a four-year school can become a junior.

A mathematics course was designed at Miami–Dade Community College to teach the necessary objectives of the math section of the CLAST. This course is necessary because of the far-reaching objectives of the computation section of the CLAST, including not only basic mathematics, algebra, and geometry but also statistics, logic, and computer technology. When it became apparent that Miami–Dade Community College students needed additional writing instruction, a third English course in advanced composition was made a graduation requirement. There was a reduction in class sizes to accommodate new writing requirements.

In conjunction with the development of the CLAST, Florida State Senator Jack Gordon proposed that the Department of Education enact what is now known as the "Gordon Rule." This rule requires the student to write, during the first two years of college, a total of 24,000 words in specific courses. The student must attain a minimum grade of C in these courses. All students must also complete two mathematics courses at the level of college algebra or higher. This rule became effective soon after our general education curriculum was established; therefore, our new curricu-

Table 3. Percent of Faculty Who Support Requiring Passing Scores Prior to Enrollment in Core Courses

General Education Core Course	Communications Faculty n=62	Mathematics Faculty n=31n	Core Faculty n=60	Other Faculty n=203	All Faculty n=356
English	92	97	97	98	96
Humanities	69	71	81	52	62
Social science	62	71	76	52	60
Natural science	68	83	83	69	72
Mathematics	95	100	95	97	97

lum had to be adjusted to fit these new mandates. Every state institution was required to identify specific courses that are now known as Gordon Rule courses. At Miami–Dade Community College, students in each of the three English composition courses must write 6,000 words, while every other general education core courses has a 1,500-word requirement.

The Effects of CLAST

Passing scores for the CLAST were established by the Department of Education. These scores were set at relatively low levels in 1983, with scheduled increases in 1986 and 1989. Faculty at the university level were not very concerned about this exam. After all, their students had already been screened and selected for potential success in college-level work. Private institutions were even less concerned, since the CLAST was required only at public institutions.

At the community colleges, however, we were quite apprehensive. The faculty's initial reaction was rejection. How could the state legislature impose an exam and then deny access to a college degree to any person on the basis of that one exam? After a while, the realization that the exam was here to stay became accepted by the majority of the faculty.

Underprepared Students. What about that very large group of students who start at community colleges at levels below those required by state universities? Would those students be able to pass the CLAST and continue their studies? At Miami–Dade Community College, approximately two-thirds of our incoming students require remediation in at least one basic skills area (Losak, personal communication, 1987). Many faculty and administrators realized that our students needed to prepare for the exam. Besides the curriculum changes mentioned earlier and the addition of a math course and a third English composition course, CLAST preparation workshops have been developed and are offered on an optional basis to students during the two weeks before administration of the CLAST. Some faculty believe that it is wrong to teach for the test, but others believe that we have a moral obligation to help our students.

Well-Prepared Students. We also have students who are eligible for admission to state universities but choose to start their college educations at community colleges. Many of these students are capable of passing the CLAST without the added English composition and math courses, but because the general education program is so directive (partly by design and partly by Department of Education regulations), these students' needs are not always met. Honors sections of the core courses and of certain distribution courses are offered regularly, but more flexibility should be allowed. Some faculty would like to see advanced placement in composition courses, so that some of these students could initially enroll in the second or third composition course. A proposal is also being considered by the Collegewide Academic Affairs Committee to let these students enroll in writing-intensive courses in the humanities or social sciences that would serve as alternatives to the third English composition course.

Meanwhile, the private universities realized that any student receiving state financial aid would be required to pass the CLAST in order to continue receiving that aid. Therefore, a larger number of students than was originally expected are now required to take the CLAST. In Miami, both the state university and a private university have contracted with Miami–Dade Community College to provide their students with the same CLAST preparation workshops in which many of our own students enroll.

When CLAST scores are released by the Department of Education, the local newspapers usually compare the results among the institutions of higher learning in South Florida. Miami–Dade Community College scores have slowly but steadily increased, to the point that our pass rate for some administrations of the test has been the highest of all the colleges and universities in Miami. We, the faculty, take pride in this accomplishment. We believe that the system now in place—combined with a very dedicated and hardworking faculty and students who are increasingly serious about their education—has made these improvements possible.

Nevertheless, we are very concerned that raising the passing scores, as was just done for the September 1986 administration of the CLAST, will prevent many students, particularly minorities, from completing their studies. This is especially worrisome at Miami–Dade Community College, since 54 percent of our students are Hispanic and 18 percent are black. A significant decrease in the percentage of students passing all four subsections of the CLAST was noted for the September 1986 administration (Montalvo, 1987).

Impact on Faculty. The past few years have been difficult. Class sizes have been reduced in the English composition and college preparatory courses, but other courses at the college have had to increase in size, since adequate funding to take care of the new demands in these courses has not been forthcoming from the state legislature. As mentioned earlier, more and more faculty must teach the college preparatory courses and the core courses instead of the more interesting elective courses. Some faculty members have had to be retrained. For example, a psychology instructor has found it necessary to take graduate courses in mathematics, and an education professor is teaching remedial reading this term.

Impact on Students. Students also have had to adjust. They are affected the most by entry/exit testing. I note a marked difference in their attitudes toward school. They are more serious and more conscious of the pressures placed on them by the CLAST. They are also more willing to accept difficult assignments if they see that these assignments will enable them to achieve success. They are not so likely to search for easy instructors, particularly in English and mathematics courses.

As we try to ensure that students are well-prepared for the last two years of college, many capable students may nevertheless ultimately be denied the opportunity to earn four-year degrees. McCabe (1987) argues that if the 1989 CLAST standards are implemented, the number of black students becoming college juniors would decrease to 10 percent and the number of Hispanic juniors would decrease to 20 percent below the 1982 level. This trend is totally unacceptable. Therefore, CLAST scores should not be used as the sole predictors of future success in college. A more balanced approach, as suggested by McCabe (1987) and by Losak and Wright (1983) would be the use of CLAST scores in conjunction with the grade point average.

References

Losak, J., and Wright, T. *Should One Variable (CLAST) Be Used to Determine Entrance to Upper Division at the State University System in Florida?* Miami, Fla.: Miami–Dade Community College, 1983.

Lukenbill, J. D., and McCabe, R. H. *General Education in a Changing Society.* Dubuque, Iowa: Kendall/Hunt, 1978.

McCabe, R. H. *The Florida College Level Academic Skills Program: A Crisis on the Horizon.* Miami, Fla.: Miami–Dade Community College, 1987.

Miami–Dade Community College. *Miami–Dade 1984 Institutional Self-Study.* 8 vols. Miami, Fla.: Miami–Dade Community College, 1985.

Montalvo, T. "College Skills Scores Drop." *The Miami Herald,* January 28, 1987, p. 1B.

Ana Alejandre Ciereszko is associate professor of chemistry at Miami–Dade Community College. She is serving a second one-year term as the South Campus Faculty Senate president, representing over 350 full-time faculty members.

Part 3.
Designing
Assessment Programs
That Work

As anyone in the political arena knows, the lessons of history are too valuable to ignore. The assessment of student outcomes has a long history, with important lessons for those concerned with designing programs for contemporary purposes. The final part of this volume offers a historical perspective, along with an alternative world view for interpreting educational inputs and outcomes. A more cooperative and humanistic model of education and society is part of the value-added philosophy for determining educational excellence. When educational gains are used as criteria of excellence, a small nonselective institution may be judged superior to a large research institution that has an international reputation. When student gains are the focus of assessment, all institutions can achieve academic excellence.

Public bodies do not need to impose their own measures of student learning to have evidence that public institutions are well run.

Assessment, Curriculum, and Expansion: A Historical Perspective

Daniel P. Resnick, Marc Goulden

In this chapter, we shall consider the relationship among assessment, curricular programs, and expansion in the history of American higher education. American higher education, in our view, has undergone two periods of rapid and stressful expansion in the last 150 years, and the second of those periods has just come to an end. During these two periods of expansion, the curriculum of undergraduate education has undergone major changes. Toward the end of each period of expansion, a movement for assessment has developed, with the goal of restoring coherence and substance to the undergraduate program.

We shall argue that American higher education is now in a post-expansion phase, analogous in some ways to that of the late 1920s and 1930s. In this phase, assessment is being called on, as it was in the past, to help establish a more effective undergraduate program after a period of rapid change and accommodation. In the current political context, marked by severe economic and fiscal problems for the nation as a whole and by a growing role for state government in higher education, the potential for historic renewal offered by assessment has been obscured. Assessment has often appeared as an externally imposed set of practices

D. F. Halpern (ed.). *Student Outcomes Assessment: What Institutions Stand to Gain.*
New Directions for Higher Education, no. 59. San Francisco: Jossey-Bass, Fall 1987.

78

designed to make educational institutions accountable to public bodies. There is no question that in a few states in this decade (six at recent count), assessment has been an instrument of public accountability, operating along lines established by legislatures, but most state accountability processes rely on traditional indicators of good management and institutional effectiveness without detailing explicit procedures for evaluating student learning. Review of programs, methods, and learning in higher education has historically been a responsibility of local faculty and administrators. In our view, it has its own independent dynamic and serves the educational purposes of reflective practice in postsecondary institutions.

Expansion in Higher Education

How should expansion in American higher education be measured? In this chapter, expansion is considered from the standpoint of three different indicators: total enrollments, institutional size, and portion of the eligible age group enrolled. The first indicator is commonly cited but of limited use. It offers a macroscopic view of the outcome of a process that has brought us from sixteen thousand to more than twelve million students in 150 years. A graph of enrollment changes over time would present a picture of soaring growth, with few nuances. A hasty and unwarranted inference might be that American education has had only one significant period of expansion, from 1951 to 1983.

In our view, indicators should be sought that portray expansion as the individual campuses of this country experienced it. From this perspective, two indicators appear especially useful. One is the portion of the eligible age group entering colleges and universities. The other is the average size of institutions. Changes in both variables have placed pressure on institutions to diversify academic programs, expand teaching staffs, and offer new courses and majors. Changes in both variables have also signaled greater difficulty in maintaining the coherence of programs.

A major source of pressure on institutions has been the need to admit new generations of college students. As they have opened enrollment, institutions have been forced to deal with the issue of equity. In a certain sense, much of the history of higher education in American may be described as a story of increasing equity. Higher education has grown from a closed corporation, which at one time extended its membership almost exclusively to white male elites for professional training, to a relatively open and varied set of institutions, which serve as the most promising route to career success in America. Increases in the portion of the eligible age group attending institutions of higher education are a rough indicator of relative change in the access extended to individuals previously barred by class, gender, race, or ethnic background.

Two Critical Periods

An analysis that relies on considering the portion of the college-age population actually enrolled in colleges and universities shows, two periods of rapid and stressful growth. They are the years 1918–1928 and 1952–1975. In the first period, the portion of eighteen- to twenty-four-year-olds attending college increased from 3.6 percent to 7.1 percent, nearly doubling in ten years. In the second period, the portion of the age group enrolled nearly trebled in twenty-eight years, increasing from 13.8 percent to 40.5 percent. Simply in terms of change rates, the two periods generated almost equal amounts of institutional stress.

The same two periods emerge as critical if we turn to the number of students on each campus as an indicator. The mean size of institutions has increased dramatically over the past 150 years but especially rapidly in these two periods. To approximate this variable roughly, we divided the number of students enrolled in all institutions by the number of institutions, for selected years beginning in 1850. By 1918, average student body was slightly more than 400; by 1928, it had grown to more than 800. In 1952, the average institutional enrollment was slightly more than 1,100; by 1975, it had grown to more than 4,000. Rate of increase in institutional size adds an important element to our concept of expansion. Like portion of the eligible age group enrolled, it is an indicator of the changing structure of institutions and of the tendency toward diversity of programs.

Shifts in Programs: The First Period of Expansion

By the early 1920s, American higher education was in its first period of intensive growth. Educators complained about the new incoherence of the curriculum, the low abilities of students, and the overcrowding of institutions. Weaver, reviewing the situation in the early 1930s, after the crest of expansion had passed, wrote of "complications which have been brought about by our overextravagant expansion of courses, our overgenerous extension of elective choice, and our overambitious attempt to accept all students and serve all masters" (1931, p. 13).

There was general agreement that colleges and universities had not been able to maintain standards and programs during expansion, even in elite institutions. Educators at Columbia noted: "The caring for new thousands of students with inadequately increased staff and budget threatened to weaken, to thin, or as some came to say, to dilute the quality of the work done. College administrators began to observe, furthermore, that many of the students whom they accepted showed neither great interest nor ability in college work" (Coss, 1931, p. 1). The fault was not entirely the students', as others argued: "Generally speaking, students have been herded into larger and larger classes, often under instructors or student assistants lacking experience" (Jones, 1933, p. 14). Some assigned more direct responsibility to the students themselves for the decline: "The average student no longer comes mainly from the cultivated classes, and therefore brings with him less of culture and intellectual ambition" (Tatlock, 1924, p. 609).

A general consensus developed by the late 1920s that the one-time president of Harvard, Charles W. Eliot, bore major responsibility for the problems as well as the achievements of contemporary higher education. He had argued for and introduced to Harvard in 1869 a program of electives, weakening the notion of an accepted core of liberal learning. At the same time, he had prepared the groundwork for an adaptive, expanding, and evolving university program. Educators were unsure whether to sing the praises of expansion, which had made institutions of higher education financially viable, or to damn the changes that had taken place in student programs. A partisan of expansion looked favorably on the role Eliot had played: "Eliot found our institutions of higher learning, in 1869, poorly attended; and he rightly judged that it was because they did not offer an attractive and effective training for American life. He believed that a revived curriculum, set into relation with our own cultural needs and open freely to the student's choice, would be sufficiently interesting and sufficiently successful in its results to attract much larger groups of students. Our registrars and our business managers can tell us how correct his belief has proved to be" (Weaver, 1931, pp. 12–13). Critics of expansion, however, saw a course program with a "fantastic patchiness which was sometimes ludicrous" (Tatlock, 1924, p. 609).

The Call for Assessment

Between the wars, essay and oral examinations were the favored formal measures of achievement. Standardized norm-referenced aptitude and subject-matter achievement tests using multiple-choice items already had gained popularity in the 1920s in the primary and secondary schools. This "new type" of examination, as it was called, penetrated higher education much more slowly, despite the hopes of its advocates (Kandel, 1936). Entrance to colleges and universities continued largely to be based, throughout the interwar period, on completion of essay examinations. Although Carl Brigham did introduce the Scholastic Aptitude Test for college applicants in 1926, essay examinations were still maintained until 1942 (Resnick, 1982; Schudson, 1972).

Comprehensive exams in the major fields or across fields, using essays and oral interrogation and modeled on English university practice, had been common in American higher education through most of the nineteenth century. By the interwar period, however, many educators had come to associate these assessment practices with an earlier era marked by a stronger common core of learning. President Lowell, Eliot's successor at Harvard, had encouraged this kind of association when he bemoaned the passing of comprehensive examinations: "The American college education was formerly based upon a fixed curriculum, comprising the studies deemed essential to liberal culture and to preparation for citizenship . . . So far as I am aware, [the comprehensive examination] has now disappeared altogether, largely on account of changes brought about by the introduction of electives of some kind" (Lowell, 1911, p. 46). Fragmentation of knowledge and of the curriculum had meant the disappearance of the comprehensive exam.

With the assistance of such examinations, educators in the interwar period hoped to restore the integrity of a lost curriculum. It was not their only strategy. Many institutions chose to restrict admissions, some to provide a more supervised and integrated undergraduate experience, others to emphasize honors programs, and many to extend their academic counseling. Restoration of the comprehensive examination for all students, however, was central to their efforts. In 1920, there were only seven institutions with two or more departments that required candidates for the baccalaureate degree to take comprehensive field examinations. By 1935, there were seventy-seven institutions with those requirements in two or more departments. (Jones, 1933, has collected data on the use of comprehensive examinations in American higher education.)

Comprehensive examinations were expected to bring integrity back to major fields of study, increase student motivation to learn, and offer students an opportunity to defend their command of a field. In the often unfavorable comparisons of American with Western European higher education, the weakness of our examination process was often cited (Kandel, 1936; Aydelotte, 1931, pp. 59–62; Flexner, 1930). For educational reformers, there is little question that assessment was intended to provide remedies for the fragmentation of the curriculum during the preceding period of expansion. Comprehensive field exams were essential elements in the "new doctrine" of reformers. They argued the following four points:

- The college student should learn to educate himself
- The student should receive stimulus and guidance from his teachers, but he needs a good deal of time to himself to accomplish his task of self-education
- The objective for the college student should be a thorough knowledge of some one field, a large subject, or a group of related subjects
- The student should be tested at the close of his college course in examinations covering the whole field of his concentrated study (Walters, 1932, p. 165).

A Second Expansion

We are currently at the end of a second period of expansion in higher education. That period lasted from 1952–1983, but its years of most intense and sustained increases in growth were 1952–1975. Like the first expansion, it was driven in part by demographic factors and in part by an increased importance assigned, in the workplace and in society at large, to additional years of education. Some of the enrollment increase can be attributed to the baby boom, the rest to an increased portion of the eligible age group attending college. The number of undergraduates in postsecondary institutions more than trebled in this period, from about 3 million in the early 1950s to more than 9.75 million students by 1983.

More than was the case in the first expansion, the structure of institutions changed as they grew larger and more varied. Large state universities became multiversities, and community colleges increased sevenfold in number. At the end of this expansion, more than 40 percent of the close to ten million undergraduate students were in two-year community colleges—part-time, older, vocationally oriented, and less likely to complete four-year degrees than the smaller portion of community college students at the beginning of this second wave of expansion. Almost all the increase in accredited colleges and universities, which grew from two thousand to more than three thousand, is due to growth in this sector (National Center for Education Statistics, 1973, 1979, 1985; Bureau of the Census, 1976).

In the baccalaureate colleges and research universities, course programs for undergraduates changed dramatically, as can be seen in the changing patterns of student majors. Student majors in the liberal arts declined precipitously. The portion of students majoring in history, philosophy, math, social science, literature, foreign languages, and science dropped from 40 percent to 20 percent. The major gainer in student majors was business. Selected as a major by 23 percent of those receiving baccalaureate degrees at the end of this second period of expansion, business had almost doubled its share of undergraduate degrees in twenty years (National Center for Education Statistics, 1985).

The nature of the college experience had been radically altered by the changes just described. Moreover, the changes had take place during a period marked at the end by a forced relaxation of the authority of college administrators over students, when there seemed to be little control over programs, achievement, and social conduct. While expansion was in progress, there was little opportunity to impose control or order over growth. By the late 1970s, however, there was a pause. Secondary institutions were the first target of public attention. Colleges and universities were next on the agenda.

The coherence of programs, the status of general education, and the competence of students are critical issues today, as they were in the late 1920s and 1930s. For Boyer (1987, p. 251), "there is growing concern that the pieces of a college education do not add up to a coherent whole." "Our college and universities," writes Bennett (1985), "must do a better job of providing a coherent and rigorous curriculum for students." A similar argument had been made a year earlier. "The realities of student learning, curricular coherence, the quality of facilities, faculty morale, and academic standards no longer measure up to our expecations" (Study Group on the Conditions of Excellence in American Higher Education, 1984, p. 8). There seems to be little disagreement that, whatever the source, there are large numbers of poorly qualified and poorly educated students who graduate from institutions of higher education. Their existence and the attention drawn to them have contributed to what has been seen as a crisis in confidence in higher education.

Assessment has been part of the response to this crises. Considering the gap between expectation and achievement as a warning signal, the Study Group on the Conditions of Excellence in American Higher Education (1984, p. 14) argued the need to move from a concern with bringing in qualified students to monitoring and improving the quality of those who actually entered: "These warning signals . . . indicate the tendency of colleges to control their 'inputs,' such as the characteristics of the students they *admit,* while paying insufficient attention to their 'outputs'—in particular, the learning of the students they *graduate.* Very few institutions actually monitor the growth of their students from entry to exit."

College Administrators' Views

We are now in the middle of a major revival of interest in assessment at the college level, of the kind we have come to expect at the end of a major period of expansion. In this section, we shall examine the kinds of assessment currently in use or enjoying the greatest approval, as reported by college administrators. Specific evidence on college administrators' perceptions of assessment comes from a recent survey conducted by the American Council on Education (El-Khawas, 1986, p. 22). Presidents and academic vice-presidents of about 450 institutions were asked the following question: "New methods of assessing student learning . . . are being discussed currently. Which of the following do you believe to be *appropriate* for your institution? Which are now *used* to assess students?"

From the data presented in this survey, we have constructed two tables. Both list the thirteen assessment measures most commonly cited by college administrators as either now in use or appropriate. Data were reported separately for three categories of institutions—universities, four-year colleges, and two-year colleges. Table 1 lists methods reported to be currently in use. Table 2 presents the growth potential for each of these measures. We have considered growth potential as the difference between measures actually in use and those considered appropriate. Measures with the greatest growth potential were judged to be those for which at least 40 percent more respondents expressed approval in each institution than did current users.

Table 1. Methods of Assessment Now In Use

	Universities	Four-Year Colleges	Two-Year Colleges
College-level skills or minimum competency tests			
Tests of general knowledge in areas such as the humanities and sciences			
Comprehensive tests in a student's major			
Tests of critical thinking			
Tests of quantitative problem solving			
Tests of oral communication			
Tests of writing		X	
Value-added measures of student gains while in college			
Mathematics placement tests for entering students	X	X	X
English placement tests for entering students	X	X	X
Reading placement tests for entering students	X	X	X
Placement tests in other skills for entering students			
Pre- and posttests for remedial courses	X	X	X

X = measures reported in use by at least 50 percent of the sample for each type of institution.
Source: El-Khawas, 1986.

With respect to current assessment measures in fairly widespread use, we note that in all three categories of institutions, four measures are commonly cited. All four, largely mathematics and English tests, are used for placement of entering students. In the case of remedial students, the placement test is given a second time after completion of the remedial course. Only in the four-year colleges do at least 50 percent of the sample report the use of writing tests.

Placement measures can be helpful to match students and faculty in courses of appropriate difficulty, establish the remedial or introductory course learning that has taken place in one's own and other institutions, and gauge minimum levels of student competency, even when placement measures are not labled as competency tests. It can be argued that placement measures include college-level skills or minimum competency tests (combined in a separate category in El-Khawas, 1986, since such tests can be used to establish eligibility for placement in junior year programs of a

Table 2. Methods of Assessment: Growth Potential

	Universities	Four-Year Colleges	Two-Year Colleges
College-level skills or minimum competency tests	X		
Tests of general knowledge in areas such as the humanities and sciences	X		
Comprehensive tests in a student's major	X	X	
Tests of critical thinking	X	X	X
Tests of quantitative problem solving	X	X	X
Tests of oral communication	X	X	X
Tests of writing		X	X
Value-added measures of student gains while in college	X	X	X
Mathematics placement tests for entering students			
English placement tests for entering students			
Reading placement tests for entering students			
Placement tests in other skills for entering students			
Pre- and posttests for remedial courses			

X = measures with growth potential of at least 40 percent by type of institution. Growth potential reflects the difference between approval for measures, as appropriate, and their actual use by type of institution.
Source: El-Khawas, 1986.

state university system). In any case, although 50 percent of the sample in each category reports using placement tests, there is no comparable constituency for tests of minimum competency.

A second category of measures involves higher-order skills—critical thinking, quantitative problem solving, and perhaps aspects of writing and oral communication. These skills are in areas where current expectation moves beyond common patterns of course experience and valid available measures. With the exception of writing (in the universities) and critical thinking (in the two-year colleges), all categories of institutions have a high growth potential for increased assessment in these areas. The four-year colleges can be expected to play the largest role in developing and using such measures.

A third category of measures involves tests of knowledge in major fields or across broad areas, such as the humanities and the sciences. While these areas are considered appropriate for development by all categories of institutions, only the four-year colleges can be expected to show major activity in them over the next decade, by our criterion of growth potential. They are the institutions that have the clearest responsibility for liberal arts programs and that see restoration of the integrity and structure of general education as close to their own missions. Four very general observations can be made:

- There are many kinds of assessment already in progress at colleges and universities
- Assessment of learning, beyond course exams, is expected to grow over the next decade
- Four-year colleges will play a leading role in this growth
- Assessment will draw increasing attention to the curriculum, and an increase in comprehensive examinations in the major fields and in testing of higher level skills, based on what has been learned at more than an introductory or remedial level, will focus more attention on the quality of the undergraduate program of studies.

Conclusion

In the middle of the first period of rapid expansion in higher education during the early 1920s, Tatlock (1924, p. 61) bemoaned the absence of assessment measures that could register the difference between the ideals of college education and the actual gains made by students. "There is no opportunity," he complained, "to appraise the student as an entire educated human being." A decade later, when the pace of expansion had slowed, many institutions were developing different kinds of integrative and holistic assessment measures, especially comprehensive examinations in the major fields. Locally devised and faculty administered, these tests nevertheless responded to a national need.

The next period of rapid and sustained growth, 1952–1983, again swept away the comprehensive examination and many of the structured features of the undergraduate program. Today, with undergraduate enrollments at a plateau, there is renewed interest in ways to strengthen the undergraduate program, motivate student effort, and gauge achievement. Eighteen institutions are now in the first year of a three-year FIPSE-sponsored effort aimed at reintroducing field examinations. (Stanley Paulson, vice-president, Association of American Colleges, is project director. The office of Ted Marchese, vice-president, American Association for Higher Education, serves as a clearinghouse for information about a variety of college assessment projects.) In the nature of this kind of experiment, efforts to gain faculty consensus on expectations for student achievement will bring into play some restructuring of undergraduate major programs.

Two major difficulties surround the current effort at reconstruction. The first deals with the knowledge explosion of the past fifty years, which has created a multitude of subdisciplines and spinoffs in every major field of inquiry. This problem will have to be addressed by every department that imposes or reimposes departmental or disciplinary examinations. It is not clear that many departments will be able to overcome the fragmentation of knowledge in their disciplines in ways that will allow them to establish clear expectations for student majors. Those that have already shaped their major programs to reflect the particular interests of subfields, rather than the full spectrum of interests in a discipline, will have the least difficulty in meeting this challenge.

The second problem is political and has to do with the relationship between academic institutions and public bodies. During the last fifty years, the dependence of higher education on public support has deepened. At the same time, competing demands of different constituencies for public dollars have increased. The search for ways to cut costs and maintain quality has led state legislatures and departments or boards of education to scrutinize the operations of public universities and colleges more closely. Under these circumstances, faculty at some institutions, who normally would carefully review their programs and the achievement of their students, have developed suspicion toward assessment. Public bodies, however, do not need to impose their own measures of student learning to have evidence that public institutions are well run. Those measures can be provided from traditional indicators of good management and institutional effectiveness. As public bodies turn away from a preoccupation with specific measures of student learning, leaving this professional responsibility to faculty, we expect to see departments and disciplines engaging more actively in assessment. The present historical conjuncture is favorable for the reconstruction of undergraduate programs. Without attention to assessment, however, reform efforts have little promise of success.

References

Aydelotte, F. "Honors Courses at Swarthmore." In H. E. Hawkes, A. C. Hanford, F. Aydelotte, L. B. Hopkins, and C. S. Boucher, *Five College Plans*. New York: Columbia University Press, 1931.

Bennett, W. J. "Foreword." In C. Adelman (ed.), *Assessment in American Higher Education: Issues and Contexts*. Washington, D.C.: Office of Educational Research and Improvement, U.S. Department of Education, 1985.

Boyer, E. L. *College: The Undergraduate Experience in America*. New York: Harper & Row, 1987.

Bureau of the Census. *Historical Statistics of the United States: Colonial Times to 1970*. 2 vols. *Washington, D.C.: U.S. Government Printing Office, 1976.*

Coss, J. J. "Introduction." In H. E. Hawkes, A. C. Hanford, F. Aydelotte, L. B. Hopkins, and C. S. Boucher, *Five College Plans*. New York: Columbia University Press, 1931.

El-Khawas, E. *Campus Trends, 1986*. Higher Education Panel Reports, no. 73. Washington, D.C.: American Council on Education, 1986.

Flexner, A. *Universities: American, English, German*. Oxford, England: Oxford University Press, 1930.

Jones, E. S. *Comprehensive Examinations in American Colleges*. New York: Macmillan, 1933.

Kandel, I. L. *Examinations and Their Substitutes in the United States*. Bulletin no. 28. New York: The Carnegie Foundation for the Advancement of Teaching, 1936.

Lowell, A. L. "Disadvantages of the Current American Practice of Conferring Degrees (with the Exception of the Ph.D.) on the Accumulation of Credits in Individual Courses, Rather Than as the Result of Comprehensive Examinations upon Broad Subjects." *Journal of Proceedings and Addresses of the Thirteenth Annual Conference, Association of American Unviersities*, 1911, pp. 45-52.

National Center for Education Statistics. *Digest of Education Statistics, 1972 Edition*. Washington, D.C.: U.S. Government Printing Office, 1973.

National Center for Education Statistics. *Digest of Education Statistics, 1979 Edition*. Washington, D.C.: U.S. Government Printing Office, 1979.

National Center for Education Statistics. *Conditions of Education, 1985 Edition*. Washington, D.C.: U.S. Government Printing Office, 1985.

Resnick, D. P. "History of Educational Testing." In A. Wigdor and W. Garner (eds.), *Ability Testing: Uses, Consequences, and Controversies. Part II*. Washington, D.C.: National Research Council, 1982.

Schudson, M. S. "Organizing the Meritocracy: A History of the College Entrance Examination Board." *Harvard Educational Review*, 1972, *42* (1), 34-69.

Study Group on the Conditions of Excellence in American Higher Education. *Involvement in Learning: Realizing the Potential of American Higher Education*. Washington, D.C.: National Institute of Education, 1984.

Tatlock, J. S. "The General Final Examination in the Major Study: Report by Committee G." *Bulletin of the American Association of University Professors*, 1924, *10*, 609-635.

Walters, R. "Honors Work, the Tutorial Method, and General Examinations." In G. M. Whipple (ed.), *Changes and Experiments in Liberal-Arts Education*. 31st Yearbook of the National Society for the Study of Education, Part 2. Bloomington, Ill.: Public School Publishing, 1932.

Weaver, W. "The New Curriculum at the University of Wisconsin." In W. Gray (ed.), *Recent Trends in American College Education. Proceedings of the Institute for Administrative Officers of Higher Institutions*. Chicago: University of Chicago Press, 1931.

Daniel P. Resnick is professor of history at Carnegie Mellon University and the author of several studies of the history of educational testing. He is currently working with Marc Goulden, a graduate research assistant, on assessment practices in postsecondary institutions. This research is supported by the Carnegie Foundation for the Advancement of Teaching.

The main problem with traditional views of excellence is that they do not directly address higher education's most fundamental purpose: the education of students.

Assessment, Value-Added, and Educational Excellence

Alexander W. Astin

As the outcomes assessment movement begins to spread into the higher education systems of many states, assessment is becoming an increasingly controversial issue. It is my impression that many of the issues concerning assessment in higher education are really issues of values, philosophy, and theory, rather than practical, nuts-and-bolts issues. At the heart of these philosophical issues is our sense of what the purpose of higher education is or should be and of what we mean when we speak of educational excellence. In this chapter, I shall discuss some of these philosophical or value questions and then try to show how they relate to more practical assessment issues.

Traditional Views of Excellence

Although quality and excellence are proabably the most fashionable terms in educational discussions these days, very few of us have taken the trouble to define exactly what we mean by excellent education. My own research suggests that despite this inattention to definition, there are several definitions of excellence that are implicit in our standard educational policies and practices.

Let us briefly review these traditional notions about excellence and then move to a consideration of the value-added approach. For simplicity, I

D. F. Halpern (ed.). *Student Outcomes Assessment: What Institutions Stand to Gain.*
New Directions for Higher Education, no. 59. San Francisco: Jossey-Bass, Fall 1987.

have found it convenient to label the traditional notions of excellence as the *reputational* and the *resources* approaches. In the reputational approach, excellence is equated with an institution's rank in the prestige "pecking order" of institutions. Since the reputational approach relies primarily on national polls and surveys, it amounts to a kind of popularity contest in which faculty members or administrators are asked to rank different types of colleges and universities in terms of their relative excellence or quality. In the resources approach, quality or excellence is equated with such things as the test scores of the entering freshmen, the endowment, the physical plant, faculty salaries, or the scholarly productivity of the faculty. Presumably, institutions that have many such resources are more excellent than those that have relatively few.

These traditional approaches to excellence are, of course, mutually reinforcing, since having a good reputation brings in additional resources, and having abundant resources helps to enhance an institution's reputation. This symbiotic relationship probably helps to explain why the reputational and the resources approaches are so popular. However, the research on student development indicates that having a great reputation and abundant resources does not necessarily guarantee excellence in the educational program; indeed, some of the most effective undergraduate education occurs at institutions with very modest reputations and resources (Bowen, 1981).

One major appeal of the resources view is that it is highly consistent with today's dominant values. We live in a highly materialistic society, in which the quality of life and individual worth are equated with material possessions. The various news media devote substantial time and space to discussions of the economy, most political candidates these days stress economic issues in their campaigning, and such publications as the *Chronicle of Higher Education* reguarly print articles and statistical summaries related to the public and private funding of higher education. Little wonder, then, that so many persons equate quality in higher education with institutional resources.

Excellence as the Development of Human Talent

The main problem with traditional views of excellence is that they do not directly address higher education's most fundamental purpose: the education of students. If we accept the idea that higher education's principal reason for being is to develop the talents of its students—or, as the economists would say, to develop the "human capital" of the nation—then the terms *quality* and *excellence* should reflect educational effectiveness, rather than mere reputation or resources. The most common label used for an approach that relies on educational effectiveness is the phrase *value-added*. Since this concept derives from a rather specialized area of economic theory, I have recently come to prefer the phrase *talent development* instead of *value-added* (Astin, 1985). *Talent development* is more educational in tone and highlights what institutions are really about: the fullest development of student potential.

It is my impression that many college faculty and most administrators, not to mention most legislators and policymakers, continue to rely on the reputational and resources approaches to excellence. Thus, their primary emphasis is on the sheer accumulation of resources. Becoming rich and famous, so to speak, becomes a kind of end in itself. Talent development, in contrast, focuses much more on the effective utilization of resources and views their accumulation simply as a means to an end, rather than as an end in itself.

If we can drop our institutional perspectives briefly and look at higher education as a total system, the reputational and resources approaches really do not serve us well. Institutions usually must compete with one another for finite resources. Let us consider the consequences. Given that there are only so many faculty "stars" to go around, and only so many students with high test scores to be recruited, all the competition in the world among institutions is not going to increase those numbers in the total system. In other words, while an institution may benefit itself if it succeeds in hiring a faculty "star" from a neighboring institution or in recruiting a National Merit Scholar from that institution, it is merely depriving its neighbor of these resources and adding nothing to the total pool. Thus, in the aggregate, competition among institutions for faculty and students does nothing to increase the excellence of the system as a whole. Because a tremendous amount of institutional time, energy, and money is spent in trying to acquire resources, one paradoxical result of relying on the resources approach to excellence is that we actually deplete them, depriving ourselves of resources that might otherwise be spent on the educational program. A similar program exists with the reputational approach. Since only so many can be top-ranked institutions, the overall excellence of the system is always constrained by the fact that if one institution succeeds in increasing its reputation, it must displace some other institution to a lower position.

Competition or Cooperation?

These zero-sum games do not apply, however, to talent development. If my faculty at UCLA manages to improve its educational programs so that students actually learn better and faster, this improvement in no way inhibits or constrains what the Berkeley or Davis campuses or any other college or university can do. In other words, with talent development, all institutions (or, for that matter, none) can be excellent. One institution's success in no way limits what any other institution can accomplish. On the contrary, when the focus is talent development, institutions can learn from one another how best to educate their students, so that one institution's success can actually be used to enhance the effectiveness of other institutions. Such a cooperative system seems far more effective in raising the educational level of the population than a system where institutions squander resources in competition for higher rankings.

In the past year I have been thinking a lot about why we have tended to favor the reputational and resources approaches to excellence, and why talent development (the value-added approach), which seems so consistent with our educational mission, has not been more widely accepted and practiced. I think the ultimate answer to this question lies mostly in the larger society and in the particular philosophical or value perspectives that hold sway at any particular time. What I really mean is our world view, our concept of the fundamental nature of human beings and of societies. The more I think about these issues, the more I am tempted to conclude that there are two fundamentally different world views that one can adopt in looking at educational as well as societal issues. For simplicity, let us characterize these as the *competitive* view and the *cooperative* view of human nature and society.

In the competitive world view, the greatest achievements of our nation are viewed as results of our intense individualism and competitiveness, and it is only through this competitive spirit that we are believed to have achieved greatness as a society. Classical free enterprise is certainly a competitive activity, in which individuals are given the maximum opportunity to vie with each other for the largest possible share of resources and rewards. This competitive world view has deep roots in the history of Western civilization, but the rise of Darwinism, with its emphasis on competition among species and survival of the fittest, provided for the first time a scientific framework in which to view the development of the human species as a competitive enterprise.

A cooperative world view offers a vastly different frame of reference. In this view, human progress and the development of society are seen as depending on the ability of individuals and groups to cooperate with one another. The survival and evolution of humankind is seen neither as a victory in the struggle with other species nor as a conquest of the environment, but rather as a manifestation of our ability to work cooperatively with one another toward common goals and to live in harmony with the environment.

While this is not the place to explore the larger social and political aspects of these two world views, it is worth noting that the cooperation-competition dichotomy symbolizes many other controversial aspects of our nation and of our world and its problems: international relations; world trade; disarmament and arms control; superpower relations; problems in the Middle East, Africa, and Latin America; guns versus butter; the welfare state versus free enterprise; and even masculinity versus femininity.

It seems to me that these world views are closely paralleled by our different views of excellence. The reputational approach is inherently competitive, since it fosters competition among institutions for higher and higher rankings. The most obvious manifestation of this competition takes place in the arena of resources, where institutions compete with one another for the largest possible share. Talent development, in contrast, is not inherently competitive, since one institution's success does not come at the expense of another's, and institutions can actually benefit from one another's successes.

Pursuing Talent Development

Accepting talent development as an approach to excellence does not automatically solve the very practical problem of how our institutions can best carry out this mission. Nevertheless, much of the research evidence on student development in higher education points to a single key ingredient in effective learning: student involvement. Basically, *involvement* refers to the amount of time and physical and psychological energy the student invests in the learning process. The greater the involvement, the greater the learning.

A couple of years ago, I had the opportunity to work with a group of six other scholars in preparing the report *Involvement in Learning* (Study Group on the Conditions of Excellence in American Higher Education, 1984). Our group worked intensely for a year, looking at all the available research evidence to determine the most effective ways of improving talent development in undergraduate education in the United States. Our report set forth a number of specific recommendations for how institutions and policymakers can best reform and strengthen undergraduate education. As suggested by the title of our report, the cornerstone of our analysis was student involvement. In the process of formulating our recommendations, however, we decided that it would be important to set forth a theory of excellence, which would provide some guidance to institutions that wished to enhance talent development. Beyond the notion of involvement, our simple theory recommended two other key elements in an excellent undergraduate education: high expectations, and assessment/feedback.

In my view, the notion of expectations is crucial to understanding the significance of involvement, since the term *expectations* really specifies the particular ends or outcomes toward which involvement is directed. In other words, it is one thing to say that a student is highly involved, and it is another to say to what end that involvement is directed. In this regard, I strongly commend to your attention the recent report *Integrity in the College Curriculum* (Association of American Colleges, 1985), which attempts to specify some of these expectations. In particular, this report emphasizes that curriculum debates should not focus exclusively on courses or course content but rather on the learning outcomes that we desire to attain through our courses. By *learning outcomes,* I mean such things as critical thinking skills, communication skills, and the like.

The third ingredient in an excellent educational environment is assessment/feedback. Basically, assessment/feedback serves two purposes. First, it is a means whereby we can make our expectations operational and explicit. It is one thing to state verbally that we want to enhance our students' communication skills, but it is quite another matter to specify, in the form of concrete assessment procedures, just what we mean by such skills. The second use of assessment/feedback is to enhance the learning process itself. This enhancement occurs in two ways. First, by obtaining a comprehensive assessment of the skills and competencies of newly admitted students, we are in an excellent position to counsel those students about curricular choices and also to design the most appropriate learning experiences. Second, assessment is used to measure growth or improvement over time by means of follow-up testing.

I want to emphasize that talent development does not depend on the use of any particular assessment method. Objective tests, essays, oral examinations, and many other approaches might be appropriate, depending on the nature of the program or the content and objectives of the course in question.

Outcomes, or Value-Added

The distinction between outcomes and value-added is often poorly understood by educators and especially by employers. The employer is really only interested in outcomes—that is, the level of developed competency or talent of the graduates of an institution. When or how the person's talents were developed to that particular level are really of no concern. Indeed, there are probably many talented high school graduates whose level of talent development is already sufficient (say, in areas such as mathematics or physics) to meet requirements of an employer. Whatever the college might add to this level of developed talent may, from the employer's perspective, be superfluous or possibly irrelevant.

This issue might be easier to understand with an example from competitive sports. Some basketball players, for example, have already developed their playing skills to a professional level before they ever enter college and, indeed, a few players have actually gone directly from high school to the professional ranks, without bothering to attend college. The Philadelphia '76ers' all-pro center, Moses Malone, is one of the more notable examples of a high school player whose talents were already so well developed that college was not deemed necessary. Whether Malone would actually have become an even better professional player by spending four years playing college basketball is a moot question, but it is difficult to see how he could play much better than he already does. Possibly, he substituted "on-the-job training" for a college education during his first few years as a professional.

Value-added, or talent development, however, highlights the importance of the student's entering level of performance or competence. Without some assessment at the entering point, there is simply no way to determine whether and to what extent the college has actually added value to the student's competence at the exit point.

Some commentators are inclined to use the term *outcomes* as synonymous with *value-added*. The implication here is that the institution can somehow take credit (or blame) for its graduating students' levels of competence. Since there is a wide body of literature showing that the outcomes level of competency of a graduating class is highly dependent on its entering level of competency, there is simply no way to determine whether outcomes are a reflection of institutional impact, entering levels of competence, or both. Talent development emphasizes the need to determine both entering and exit levels of competency.

In passing, it may be worth pointing out that assessment in the elementary and secondary schools relies almost entirely on simple outcomes measures. Most public school districts in this country regularly administer standardized achievement tests to their students, and the mean scores of these tests are often published in local newspapers on a school-by-school basis. These outcomes measures are then used to make judgments about the comparative quality of the schools. Presumably, the schools whose students make the highest average scores are the best and, conversely, the schools whose students make the lowest average scores are the worst. Whether the highest-scoring schools can actually take credit for the good performance of their students, and whether the lowest-scoring schools can be blamed for their students' relatively poor performance, is another question. Without information on the students' performance levels at the time of their entry into the schools, there is simply no way to interpret simple outcomes measures. Obviously, the elementary and secondary schools could learn a lot more about the effectiveness of their programs and the relative effectiveness of different schools if they were to use the concept of talent development in their approach to assessment.

Improving Assessment Practices

In trying to design an effective program of assessment based on value-added, perhaps the most important thing to keep in mind is the necessity for basing that program on some coherent philosphy of the institution's mission. In particular, the assessment program should reflect some conception of what constitutes effective performance of that mission. A philosophy of the institution's purpose and mission is not just an abstract intellectual exercise; it has concrete implications for how one views the assessment program. Given a reputational and resources philosophy, for example, we would concentrate our energies and attention on assessing the level of competence of our entering students. The higher the performance at the time of entry, the more excellent the institution. Similarly, with a reputational or a simple outcomes approach, we would focus our attention on the performance of the exiting student or the graduate, as reflected in standardized tests, rates of admission to graduate school, earnings, or the number of famous graduates we have. With a philosophy of talent development, however, we would require both types of assessment—entry and exit—and gauge our effectiveness in terms of the amount of growth or improvement shown by students as a result of our educational programs. Note that talent development does not preclude the use of the other two approaches: One can always use the pretest to look at excellence in resources terms, and one can always use the posttest to look at excellence in outcomes terms, but the combination of the two assessments really allows us to look at the effectiveness of the educational program itself.

Different philosophies of institutional mission also result in different uses of assessment in higher education. Under traditional conceptions of excellence, assessment is used primarily to sort and screen students, rather than to find out how much they are actually learning. Testing and grading, in other words, are used more to compare students with one another than to chart the learning of the individual student over time. Indeed, with the possible exception of diagnostic testing, most assessment in American higher education has little to do with the educational process. It is used instead to serve the reputational and resources views of excellence. The sorting-and-screening approach actually leads to a great deal of waste in the assessment process. We test applicants for admission with one set of instruments, use another set to place new freshmen in appropriate courses, use another large and diverse set to measure performance in specific classes, and use still another set to measure competency for admission to graduate or professional school. More and more institutions around the country are using yet another set of assessment devices to measure junior or senior year competency in such fields as writing, general education, and the major. Given that most of these assessments involve different methods of test construction and scoring, it is nearly impossible to link them in order to measure change or growth in students' cognitive development.

A Theory of Utilization

Assuming that we have introduced an assessment program based on value-added, we are faced with another practical question: How can assessment actually be used to improve educational practice? To answer this question, it is first necessary to develop some theoretical conception of how administrators and faculty members operate effectively and of how students learn and develop.

I have found it convenient to view the educational practitioner as a kind of performing artist. It is important to realize that for performing artists to develop appropriate skill and technique, they must view the results of their work. The young painter sees what comes out on the canvas and makes appropriate adjustments. Aspiring musicians here what they play or sing and adjust their behavior accordingly. What I am talking about here is feedback.

Following this analogy, let us examine the traditional practices of college teachers and administrators. If their primary objective is to maximize talent development in their students, then learning how to perform this task effectively requires some type of feedback with which they can gauge the effectiveness of their efforts. If we look at the types of feedback that most teachers and administrators receive, it seems that they really have no good basis for judging the effectiveness of their efforts. They are, in effect, like artists learning to paint blindfolded, or like musicians learning to play instruments with their ears plugged.

College faculty members, as they practice the performing art of teaching, do receive informal feedback from their students in the form of classroom comments, but this feedback rarely provides systematic information on how much and how well each student is actually learning. Professors might argue that their final examinations allow them to evaluate the quality of learning, but in many respects relying on final examinations is like closing the barn door after the horse has escaped. Indeed, final examination performance is very difficult to evaluate without some clear notion of how well students performed at the beginning of a course. Some high-performing students may actually have known the material before they ever took the course. Others, with lower final examination scores, may actually have learned a great deal, considering their lack of knowledge at the beginning of the course. As for advising activities, professors rarely have the opportunity to learn about their successes and failures in this important enterprise.

Our analogy can also be extended to administrators and staff. Many areas of institutional functioning directly affect students' talent development: registration, orientation, financial aid, housing, food services, parking, social activities, career counseling, personal counseling, extracurricular activities, health services, and job placement. How can the personnel responsible for these diverse services improve their programs and policies unless they solicit systematic evaluation of their efforts from the students they serve?

In this regard, it is important to realize that faculty and administrators also need some theory to guide their efforts. I find the involvement theory extremely useful in my own work with students. The involvement concept suggests, among other things, that any assessment program should attempt to determine how much time and energy students are actually investing in the educational experience.

One particularly appealing feature of using talent development as an approach to assessment is that it provides perhaps the ideal means of maintaining academic standards. For example, if skill in written composition is a requirement for the bachelor's degree, and if an institution's current assessment program includes a test of composition skill given during the junior or senior year, that same test can be used productively in a developmental context. Thus, if the same instrument were administered to new students when they entered, this pretest would provide a clear indication of how much students would have to improve in order to reach graduation standards. Such a pretest provides invaluable information to students, advisers, and professors concerning how much distance the student must travel.

Of course, the developmental principle can also be used in individual courses. The pretest, in this case, might also be the final course examination, which would give students a much more concrete idea of what would be expected of them in terms of demonstrated knowledge or competency at the end of the course. Differences in performance between the pretest and the final examination thus could provide a basis for understanding to what extent the course had been successful in developing the desired knowledge and skill.

Practical Suggestions for Conducting Assessments

I shall now propose a number of practical suggestions for implementing a comprehensive program of value-added assessment.

The notion of pretesting and posttesting immediately conjures up the image of multiple-choice tests given repeatedly to measure talent development. Indeed, I think this stereotyped image is what most alienates faculty who are disturbed by the call for more and better assessment or for value-added assessment. There is no doubt that traditional multiple-choice testing is not appropriate for assessing what students are learning in certain fields. Thus, let us consider some other approaches.

At first glance, it might appear that the most inappropriate fields for assessment and value-added analysis are the fine and performing arts. On close inspection, however, it turns out that these are the very fields where assessment not only is an integral part of the educational process but also has been developed to a very high level of complexity. Students learning how to paint, draw, dance, compose, sing, or play instruments are continually and regularly assessed, not only by teachers but also by peers, who regularly listen to or watch their performances and provide evaluative feedback.

It is important to realize that these regular assessments in the arts are done not so much to judge, grade, evaluate as to provide feedback to the learner as a means of improving the learning process—to facilitate the development of the student's competence and talent. We should also recognize that this assessment is essential for teachers as well, in order for them to know how students are progressing and to guide the teaching-learning process.

Perhaps the only thing missing from the assessment procedures typically used in the fine and performing arts is quantification. Although it may seem like a trivial or needless exercise, putting numbers on judgments of artistic performance can serve a variety of useful purposes. Juries are used to quantify musical performance—for example, in music competitions—and such assessments can be multidimensional. A singer's performance can be judged in terms of voice quality, intonation, range, control, interpretive sensitivity, originality, and so on. At a minimum, teachers of fine and performing arts could quantify their assessments along a simple scale (ranging, say, from "beginner" to "world-class professional"), or performance could be compared before and after a particular course or other instructional program as a way of seeing how much improvement had occurred.

The usual justifications given for state-mandated assessments are to make institutions more accountable to the public and to ensure excellence and quality control in educational programs. Let us first consider the accountability argument. What is usually missing from this argument is any indication of what the state is supposed to do once the results are in. For example, if an assessment program shows that an institution's students are not substantially improving their writing skills during college, what is the state supposed to do? Should it punish the institution by withdrawing funds? Is such action likely to remedy the problem? What if the institution argues that it needs more funds in order to give professors release time to critique more frequent written assignments and essay examinations? If funds are withdrawn, then the institution may be tempted to shortchange some other important area of learning and focus more of its faculty resources on the teaching of writing. Such a trade-off may or may not be desirable, and its educational consequences may not be detectable unless the institution happens to have an assessment system that is comprehensive and sophisticated enough to reflect the performance decrement (in some other skill area, such as math) that accompanies the trade-off.

A similar problem occurs with monetary rewards for good performance. If an institution gets additional funds because its writing program is successful, it may be tempted to divert even more resources into that program, to the detriment of other important institutional offerings.

These difficulties with a simple system of rewards and punishments become even more serious when we consider competencies other than writing (which presumably can be assessed with some confidence through a writing sample). Let us say that the state mandates a test of American history, to be administered on a value-added basis in all public institutions. If monetary rewards are tied to improvements in scores, most institutions will first take a hard look at test content and then "teach to the test." An obvious consequence of this procedure would be a homogenization of history courses taught across the different public campuses. Thus, if a history department happens to have a professor who is one of the world's experts on the Civil

War, and if the state-mandated history test happens to give only cursory treatment to the Civil War, then students will be deprived of an opportunity to learn the best that this professor has to teach. Also, if the test is a multiple-choice test (which it is highly likely to be), history departments will be tempted to overemphasize the student's acquisition of mere facts and to give insufficient attention to developing the student's ability to synthesize, write creatively, and think critically about history. In short, a policy of simple rewards and punishments may not be a productive approach to state-mandated assessments in higher education.

Another possible state response to mandated assessments might be called the remedial approach. Instead of punishing poor performance, the remedial approach would provide more resources to poorer-performing institutions on the grounds that their programs are most in need of strengthening. The remedial approach is thus a kind of mirror image of the reward-and-punish approach, since the poorest-performing institutions are given more resources, rather than fewer. The problems with this approach, however, are obvious: Institutions will be tempted to encourage their students to "fake bad" in order to garner more resources. The remedial approach actually encourages institutions to "look bad" on the posttest, while the reward-and-punish approach creates incentives for them to "look bad" on the pretest. Neither model, it seems, serves the state's interest in getting more talent development out of its higher education system.

To my mind, the best kind of performance-based funding rewards good practice, such that institutions are provided with incentives to develop good data bases, conduct more and better value-added assessments, use the results in planning, increase faculty-student contact, use more active modes of learning in the classroom, and employ more pedagogical innovations. We already know much about what constitutes good practice in higher education, and any state incentive system should be designed to encourage such practice.

Part of the dilemma posed by performance-based funding results from its competitive nature. We are usually playing a zero-sum game when it comes to performance-based funding, and so one institution's success depletes the resources available to other institutions. Colleges are rooting for each other to fail.

What has not yet been considered by any state, so far as I know, is a cooperative system of performance-based funding, in which monetary incentives are based on the aggregate performance of an entire system. Under such a cooperative model, institutions would have maximum incentive to facilitate one another's performance, since the success of any one brings in resources that are shared by all the others. It is interesting to consider how relations among institutions might change under such a cooperative system of incentives.

Be Informative Rather Than Adversarial. I have already suggested that a program of institutional outcomes assessment is likely to be useful if it employs talent development as an approach to excellence, rather than the traditional reputational and resources approaches. I believe that these traditional views of excellence are inherently competitive and therefore adversarial. Who has the brightest students? Who has the most illustrious faculty? Who has the largest library? This competitive approach is further reflected in the ways traditionally used to assess students: the grade point average is a relativistic measure, which pits students against one another. Students are tested and graded to determine whether they should be admitted, awarded credit, or permitted to graduate, rather than to determine how much and how well they are actually learning. This attitude also spills over into our attempts to assess faculty members. Most assessments of faculty performance are designed to determine whether they should be hired, promoted, or given tenure. Under such conditions, the institution's assessment program is bound to be perceived as a threat. Further, this adversarial view of assessment tends to put students and faculty members into passive roles: Students and professors submit to the assessment process and try to show themselves in the most favorably light possible.

In contrast, the concept of talent development and its associated notion of involvement demand a very different purpose of assessment. In this case, assessment is used primarily for feedback, to increase the involvement of students and faculty members and to develop their talents as completely as possible. Such assessment is active rather than passive, since it is designed to facilitate and improve performance, rather than merely to evaluate it. Furthermore, the information gathered is used to benefit the parties involved, rather that to pass judgment on them.

Build on What You Already Have. Talent development in assessment does not necessarily require institutions to embark on entirely new programs of testing and evaluation. For example, most institutions already employ some kind of admissions testing program, and many also use various types of placement tests. On the basis of talent development, these admissions and placement tests can be viewed as pretests, which, together with subsequent follow-up assessments (posttests), can provide longitudinal measures of change or growth in student competency. At the same time, upper-division competency tests (in writing, basic academic skills, and related areas), which have become increasingly popular and have even been mandated in some public institutions, might provide important posttests, and students could be pretested with the same or similar devices upon entry into the institution. These pretests on upper-division competency, incidentally, can also be important guides for effective placement and counseling. Indeed, it may well be that pretesting students with upper-division competency tests at the time of entry could replace currently used admissions or placement tests, thereby obviating the need for any increase in the amount of assessment.

Perhaps the most important existing assessments to be elaborated in a context of talent development are classroom examinations. Most undergraduate courses involve some kind of final examination, and many also involve midterm exams of various types. In most cases, the same (or parallel) exams could be given to new students when they enroll in a course, thereby providing a baseline against which to measure change in the midterm and final examinations. An important additional benefit from such pretesting in the classroom is that it gives students a very concrete idea of what is expected in the course and of how much growth they must demonstrate in order to reach acceptable performance standards.

Be Opportunistic. The practical problems involved in large-scale institutional assessment of student competency should not be underestimated. The time of students and faculty members is at a premium in most institutions, and any additional assessments that would be required to implement talent development should be incorporated with minimal intrusion on faculty and student time and energy.

Many institutions fail to realize that once students begin to attend classes, it may be extremely difficult to find a way to conduct pretest assessments. It is important to realize that the student who is in the process of matriculating for the first time is generally in an extremely cooperative frame of mind and is therefore an ideal subject for pretest or placement assessments. Thus, it makes sense to capitalize on this opportunity as fully as possible and to include as many assessments as might be needed for a full-fledged program. Follow-up assessments are almost inevitably more difficult, since students may never again congregate in a single place at the same time and in the same cooperative frame of mind. Some institutions may well find it necessary to mandate follow-up postttest assessments. In states where some kind of mandatory upper-division competency assessment (such as the writing requirement at the California State University) is already in place, this posttest assessment might also be seen as an occasion to include other posttests, as appropriate. In short, institutions should attempt to identify points in the student's institutional experience where assessments are likely to be least intrusive and most acceptable to the larger academic community.

Be More Absolute and Less Relative. Almost all the widely used aptitude and achievement tests in higher education share similar test design and construction: A list of multiple-choice test items is developed and administered to a sample of students. The number of items answered correctly (possibly with adjustments for wrong answers) is calculated for each student and then converted into a derived measure, such as a standard score or a percentile score. This conversion process basically wipes out the fundamental information about how many or what percent of questions the students answered correctly, which questions were answered correctly, and so on. Instead, it provides only relativistic information derived from the normal curve and reflects only how one student has performed relative to others.

While such relative measures are used almost universally in our large-scale national and state examinations, they present some potentially serious problems. Besides indicating nothing about the student's absolute level of performance, such relativistic scores give no information about how difficult the items were or what the student's test performance implies about potential for performing well on the job, profiting from further education, and the like. More important, such relative measures offer no way of reflecting changes in the student's performance over time. Thus, it is possible for a student's absolute (actual) level of performance or competence to improve considerably over time, while his or her relative performance remains the same or even declines during the same period.

There are several possible ways to develop measures of absolute performance from the types of multiple-choice items usually found on aptitude or achievement tests, but perhaps the most straightforward approach is simply to record the number of items answered correctly. Change or growth in the student's development can thus be assessed in terms of increases in the number or percentage of items answered correctly. One useful elaboration of this approach is to develop expectancy tables that show the probability of various events (graduating on time, graduating with honors, performing well on the job, and so forth) as a function of the number of items correctly answered. Change or growth can then be measured in terms of increases in these probabilities over time.

Another method is to label particular points on the distribution of scores (whether raw or derived) in terms of the level of performance typical of that point. For example, if one were interested in using an outcomes measure of writing skill to certify students for graduation, the lowest scores might indicate borderline literacy and the highest scores might correspond to the level of writing competence required of students pursuing Ph.D.-level education. The significance of the particular scale points would be made even clearer if examples of actual items were used to show the most difficult types of items passed by the majority of people scoring at a particular point on the scale.

Get More from Your Standardized Tests. Given the heavy use of standardized tests by most colleges and universities, it is unfortunate that so little of the information collected in these tests is actually used for educational purposes to enhance talent development. One way to enhance the educational usefulness of such instruments is to obtain information concerning the student's raw scores, as well as standardized or derived scores. Such information is readily available from the testing organizations and should be requested by all institutions that utilize these tests for admissions, placement, or other purposes.

Another potentially more important type of information is the student's performance on individual test items. If it were possible to know how our students perform on individual items—which ones they find most difficult and which ones they find relatively easy—such information would be invaluable in curriculum evaluation and planning.

Testing companies have resisted providing performance information on individual test items, on the grounds that such information is unreliable. This objection may be valid in the case of individual students, but it is not really relevant to information that could be provided in aggregate form. That is, it would be extremely valuable to faculty members to know how a group of students performed on each test item. Again, testing organizations should be able to provide such information at relatively little additional cost.

Another objection to the provision of data on individual test questions concerns the need to protect test security. This argument is really a weak one, given the theory underlying the construction of most achievement tests. Briefly, the items for such tests are selected from a hypothetical domain of all possible test questions that could be asked about a particular subject. If providing item feedback to institutions violates the security of a particular set of items, then the testing company can simply write new items each year. If the domain is finite, then once all possible test items have been written and made public, the company can simply sample randomly from this domain in constructing a new test each year. It might be argued that under these conditions, professors will simply encourage their students to study for the test by learning the answers to all the items. What would be wrong with that? If the student knows the answers to all possible questions that could be used about a particular body of knowledge, then that student knows, by definition, that body of knowledge.

By obtaining access to results for individual test questions on an instrument such as the Scholastic Aptitude Test, institutions can repeat some of these tests after one, two, or four years to measure improvement in students' performance on specific items. Moreover, if the testing organizations could be persuaded to perform equating studies, whereby various instruments are equated, the results of these tests could also be used to measure improvements in cognitive performance during the undergraduate years.

While such changes in the testing organizations' feedback may be difficult for an individual institution to bring about, it should not be too difficult for several institutions that are members of regional associations or public systems to join in requesting such modifications from the testing organizations. Under such pressure, there is a good likelihood that the testing organizations will be forthcoming with the requested data.

Start Simply. For institutions that have not already established comprehensive assessment, it is important to initiate any new outcomes assessment modestly and with minimal disruption of institutional activities. A more comprehensive and complete system can evolve from these modest beginnings.

Comprehensive assessments of students' cognitive development are often resisted by institutions because of high costs and logistical problems. This resistance can be compounded by the fact that assessments of this type require a substantial lapse of time between pretest and posttest before any useful information on student growth and development is obtained. One shortcut method, which can provide useful information almost immediately, is the use of so-called surrogate measures of student cognitive development. Thus, questionnaires can be administered to students that involve three kinds of questions: self-reports about how much students think they have actually improved their skills and knowledge in various areas (a kind of "quick and dirty" assessment after the fact); student ratings of a wide range of university experiences and services, including classroom teaching, counseling, residential facilities, and so forth; and time diaries, in which students provide information about their levels of involvement in various activities by indicating how much time they spend studying, discussing subject matter with students and faculty, and so on. All three of these kinds of information can be obtained in a single questionnaire administered to students at any time during the undergraduate years. The results of such assessments can be analyzed rapidly and disseminated to faculty, staff, students, and others who have an interest in the results. A national program that produces normative information on such matters is the Follow-Up Student Survey (FUSS) conducted by the Higher Education Research Institute at UCLA (Green, Astin, Korn, and McNamara, 1983).

Getting Started. If your institution does not have a well-established tradition of longitudinal student assessment, it's important to begin to develop such a system in a modest way. A minimally useful student data base should incorporate the following core elements.

1. *Successful completion of a program of study.* In its simplest form, this measure involves a dichotomy: The student either completes a program or drops out. More sophisticated approaches to this measure involve determining whether a student's undergraduate achievements are consistent with his or her degree plans at college entry.

2. *Cognitive development.* The basic purpose of this category of information is to determine whether the institution is achieving its basic instructional purpose: to develop the cognitive abilities of its students. The surrogate measure of longitudinal cognitive development—the student's self-report of learning in various subjects—seems a modest way to start. Ultimately, of course, it is important to incorporate actual assessments of pretest and posttest cognitive performance in areas relevant to the curriculum.

3. *Student involvement and satisfaction.* Students' satisfaction with an institution's program is one of the most important indications of the institution's effectiveness. Students should be asked not only about their overall satisfaction but also about their satisfaction with more specific matters: the quality of teaching, advising, curriculum, facilities, extracurricular

activities, and various student services. Perhaps the best way to assess involvement, as suggested above, is to ask students to keep time diaries indicating how much time (per week, for example) they spend on various activities (studying, interacting with one another and with professors, working at an outside job, engaging in athletics and other activities, and so forth).

Conclusion

It is important to realize that there is nothing inherently competitive about measurement and assessment, even though most assessment in higher education is currently done in a competitive framework. Undergraduate admissions testing is done to identify the "best" students. Testing for admission to graduate or professional schools is done for the same purpose: to separate the best from the worst. Traditional course grades are almost purely competitive, producing only information on how students compare to one another and virtually nothing about what students have learned, what they do or do not know, or what competencies they have and to what degree. These course grades in turn are aggregated into grade point averages, which are used to sort and screen students and identify the best performers for graduate schools and employers. Even the more recent entries into the testing field—competency testing at the secondary level and, more recently, competency testing at the higher level—take place in a competitive framework, to determine who is eligible to pass and who is not.

The real question here is whether we are going to promote a competitive philosophy, in which assessment is viewed as adversarial and normative, and where it is used primarily to promote the reputational and resources views of excellence. In contrast, we should embrace a cooperative philosophy, in which assessment is viewed as informative and facilitative, and where it is used to enhance talent development? From the perspective of talent development, an excellent institution facilitates maximum intellectual and personal growth in its students and regularly documents that growth through appropriate assessment procedures. The choice is ours.

References

Association of American Colleges. *Integrity in the College Curriculum.* Washington, D.C.: Association of American Colleges, 1985.

Astin, A. W. *Achieving Educational Excellence: A Critical Assessment of Priorities and Practices in Higher Education.* San Francisco: Jossey-Bass, 1985.

Bowen, H. R. "Cost Differences: The Amazing Disparity Among Institutions of Higher Education in Educational Costs per Student." *Change,* 1981, *3,* 21–27.

Green, D. E., Astin, A. W., Korn, W. S., and McNamara, P. P. *The American College Student, 1982.* Los Angeles: Higher Education Research Institute, 1983.

Study Group on the Conditions of Excellence in American Higher Education. *Involvement in Learning: Realizing the Potential of American Higher Education.* Washington, D.C.: National Institute of Education, 1984.

Alexander W. Astin is professor of psychology and director of the Higher Education Research Institute at the University of California, Los Angeles.

Whatever the reasons for initiating an outcomes assessment program, all successful programs share several crucial features to success.

Recommendations and Caveats

Diane F. Halpern

As seen in the previous chapters, there is considerable diversity in the way state legislatures and individual institutions have designed outcomes assessment programs. Because of basic differences among universities and intended uses of data, there can be no single standard or prototype program, but there are common issues that need to be considered in planning and implementing any outcomes-focused assessment program. Two primary questions that need to be resolved early in the planning process are "What do you want to know?" and "Why do you want to know it?" Clear and succinct answers to these questions will provide direction to the secondary questions, "What should you measure?" and "How should you measure it?" If the purpose of student outcomes assessment is to determine what and how much students learn while at your institution, then an essential step in the planning process is deciding what you want your students to know and be able to do when they complete the academic program.

In other words, you need to have clear objectives before you can determine whether your institution has achieved them. It is useful to have faculty and administrators carefully consider the essential competencies and proficiencies that students should acquire as part of their education in their majors and/or in the general education portion of the program. The selection of appropriate measurement instruments is much easier if you know

D. F. Halpern (ed.). *Student Outcomes Assessment: What Institutions Stand to Gain.*
New Directions for Higher Education, no. 59. San Francisco: Jossey-Bass, Fall 1987.

clearly what you want to measure. If, for example, you want students to be able to present persuasive arguments or be able to explain major theories or controversies in their fields, then standardized multiple-choice tests will be unable to assess how well these objectives were obtained. If the goal is to determine how well your graduates meet the performance of graduates from other universities, then standardized multiple-choice tests with extensive norms would be the instrument of choice.

In planning a program for your institution, you should consider the following important factors.

1. Multiple and varied measures are always more desirable than a single standardized examination. A good mix would include nationally normed instruments (for example, the ACT COMP), examinations prepared by local faculty (for example, senior comprehensive exams), and readily available measures that are typically kept by institutional research offices (for example, scores on nationally normed entry exams, grade point averages, retention rates, and alumni surveys).

2. Faculty involvement in and support of all aspects of the program are essential components of success. External, top-down pressures often meet skepticism and resistance. If the main purpose of assessment is program improvement, then those responsible for shaping the curriculum must be involved in the procedures used to assess its effectiveness.

3. Performance-based funding should be derived from additional resources. Any plan to tie major portions of campus funding to performance measures is likely to result in conflict, both among and within the segments of higher education. If a performance incentive is used, the funds should supplement those generated through the usual funding formulas and should be limited to a relatively small proportion of each campus's general operating budget.

4. Outcomes assessment should be used for program decision making but is an inappropriate measure for retention and tenure decisions about faculty. Faculty and administrative goodwill is essential to the successful use of the information that outcomes assessment provides.

5. The types of data collected should reflect the campus master plan. Different sorts of outcomes can be expected from an institution that has made a commitment to liberal arts education than from one that has made research a major component of its mission. Individual campuses must have the flexibility to determine how outcomes assessment can best be achieved.

6. Value-added or talent-development measures that emphasize educational gains are preferable to exit-only data (for example, GRE scores) because they measure growth during the college years, and not just a level of achievement at graduation.

7. Most campuses are already doing a considerable amount of outcomes assessment. Unfortunately, much of it is fragmented and cannot provide a comprehensive evaluation of program or campus effectiveness. Good

assessment designs are programmatic and coordinated. They require careful planning or campuswide activities.

8. A program of outcomes assessment will cost money, especially during its first year of operation. Specific funding will be needed to cover the costs of data collection and analysis if an institution is expected to undertake a campuswide effort to assess its effectiveness.

Summary

There are many potential benefits of assessing educational outcomes, but a hastily executed or rigid program can present misleading or worthless information and create ill will, all at considerable cost. It is hoped that a thoughtful consideration of the issues presented in this volume will ensure successful outcomes assessment programs that can be used to improve teaching and learning at every institution.

Diane F. Halpern is interim dean of undergraduate studies and professor of psychology at California State University, San Bernardino. She served as chair for the October 1986 conference entitled "Student Outcomes Assessment: A Tool for Improving Teaching and Learning," sponsored by the California State University.

Index

A

Accreditation, 1, 3, 36, 43, 55

Administrators and staff: impact of assessment on, 33, 55-56, 83, 97-98; roles of, 37-42, 47-48

Alumni surveys, and assessment, 3, 15-16, 20-21, 27, 38-39, 110

Alverno College, Milwaukee, 19-20, 23, 37, 59

American Association for Higher Education, 86

American Council on Education, 83

American higher education expansion cycles and assessment, 2, 77-87

Assessment initiatives, 3, 5-7, 12-13, 25-28, 77-78, 87; government and institutional, 2-3, 23, 25-28, 29-31, 33, 67, 70-72, 80-81, 86-87, 89-106, 109; national task forces, 36-37; problems of mandated, 26, 28, 30-31, 43, 58-60, 64, 71-73, 99-100. *See also* State and assessment activities

Assessment input and outcomes: academic discipline-level, 13, 18-19, 33, 40-41, 50, 53-55, 80-81, 85-86, 105; content and prioritizing of, 10, 13-16; entrance, 3, 7, 11, 20-21, 27, 61, 68, 84, 94-96, 98, 100-101; exit, 3, 7, 13, 27, 38, 61-64, 75, 83, 86, 94-96, 100-101; general education and basic skills, 13-14, 18, 38, 58-64; institution-level, 12, 41, 53, 58-64; longitudinal, 23, 50, 53-55, 101; multiple instrument and triangulation model of, 46, 49, 57-64; program-level, 11-12; sex-linked, 63; standardized and nationally normed, 16-19, 26, 39, 50-55, 58-64, 60*f*, 110; student behavior survey, 15-16, 22, 48-50; student-level, 11, 19-20, 22, 105; surveys and questionnaires, 20-22, 27, 38-39, 49, 54, 105-106

Assessment input subject areas: arts and esthetics, 3, 60, 62, 98-99; cognitive skills, 3, 53, 84-85, 105; computer literacy, 14, 25, 70; English and writing, 26, 53, 60, 62, 68-72, 84-85; mathematics, 26-27, 60, 68-72, 84; practical and problem-solving skills, 14-15, 19-20, 25, 38-41, 60, 62, 85; prioritizing of, 10, 13-16; professional skills, 14, 17, 19, 49, 52-53; research skills, 14, 51, 60; social sciences, 17, 49, 53-54, 60-62; student religious and ethical values, 14-16, 60, 62

Assessment outcomes significance: and alumni surveys, 3, 15-16, 20-21, 110; and behavior tracking, 15-16, 22, 48-50; and data uses, 7, 20-22, 33, 39-41, 50-56, 109-110; and evaluation, 25-28, 40-43, 45, 58-64, 75; and grade-point averages, 22, 26, 50, 73, 101, 106, 110; and strategic planning, 3, 110-111. *See also* Curriculum evaluation

Assessment-based comparisons, 11, 81; and the competition-cooperation dichotomy, 92-93, 100, 106; and institutional competition, 12, 26, 28, 42, 72, 75, 100; instrument-related, 17, 19, 110; and talent development, 91-106

Association of American Colleges, 36, 43, 86, 93, 106

Astin, A. W., 2, 6, 50, 56, 89, 91, 105, 105, 106, 107

Ausebel, D., 53, 56

Aydelotte, F., 81, 87

B

Banta, T. W., 11, 19, 24, 35-36, 39, 43, 47-48, 56

Bennett, W. J., 82, 87

Bowen, H. R., 13, 24, 90, 106

Boyer, E., 31

Boyer, E. L., 82, 87

Brigham, C., 80